MW00462675

PEOPLE • PASSION • PERSISTENCE

LEAD
IN
LIFE

Succeed in the New Era of
DIVERSITY, EQUITY, and **INCLUSION**

DR. LAURA MURILLO

Lead in Life, People. Passion. Persistence
Succeed in the New Era of Diversity, Equity, and Inclusion

Dr. Laura Murillo
Houston, TX 77023
DrLauraMurillo.com

In association with:
Elite Online Publishing
63 East 11400 South #230
Sandy, UT 84070
EliteOnlinePublishing.com

LCCN: Cataloging-in-Publication Data

978-1-7377284-1-2 (Hardback)
978-1-7377284-6-7 (Paperback)
978-1-7377284-0-5 (Amazon)
978-1-7377284-7-4 (eBook)

Printed in the United States of America

First Edition

For additional content visit:
DrLauraMurillo.com

This book is a tribute to my parents,
José and Tomasa González.

To my daughters, Marisa and Mia Murillo.

"You are smart, you are beautiful, and God loves you."
Love, Mommy

Praises for Dr. Laura Murillo

"Dr. Laura Murillo is a transformational leader, motivator, and visionary.

Internationally acclaimed for her many accomplishments, she is a constant source of encouragement for young people moving into leadership positions and for seasoned entrepreneurs seeking to deepen their involvement in the wider community.

The youngest of nine children of Mexican immigrant parents, Dr. Murillo conveys authenticity and depth of experience that inspires a broad-based commitment to help Houston develop into a truly equitable and inclusive multi-ethnic community, positioned to serve as a model for all of America as the twenty-first century unfolds."

Stephen L. Klineberg, Ph.D.
Professor Emeritus of Sociology, Rice University

"Dr. Laura Murillo is a Houston treasure with national and international influence. Her expertise in diversity, equity, and inclusion has opened many doors for others. She is a force of nature with boundless energy and has a proven track record of getting things done. We are proud to partner with Dr. Laura."

Tilman Fertitta, Owner, Houston Rockets
Chairman, CEO, and Owner, Landry's, Inc.

"As President of the 2026 FIFA World Cup Houston Bid Committee, I have counted on our diverse board in assisting us in bringing the international event to Houston. Dr. Murillo serves on the board and has utilized her media and business savvy to position us for maximum exposure. Her international connections and her commitment as a board member is commendable. As President, I can count on her to bring valuable insight and knowledge on a variety of topics including diversity, equity and inclusion."

Chris Canetti
President, Houston's 2026 FIFA
World Cup Bid Committee

"Dr. Laura Murillo is a champion, advocate, and relentless leader who ensures that DEI is at the forefront of equipping and empowering the next generation of leaders.

My mentor, Dr. Murillo, continues to be a voice of reason, an inspiration to me and to countless others. Dr. Murillo encouraged me to follow my passion by leaving corporate America and diving into education to pursue my doctorate. She served as a constant reminder of my own "why". Resonating with her personal story empowered me to achieve my own goals.

From entry-level roles to the C-suite, shared experiences, shared values, and shared identities matter. Leaders such as Dr. Murillo genuinely understand this and advocate for themselves, others, and our collective impact, which creates sustainable success.

Young professionals benefit from seeing their potential and knowing they, too, can dream and achieve. Dr. Murillo serves as an example of a servant leader who has global impact and local connectivity all in one."

Dr. Ricardo Rodriguez
Director of National Programs, Latinos for Education
GHHCC Foundation, Emerging Leader Institute Graduate

"Dr. Laura Murillo has traveled across the globe representing our region with myself and other business leaders. She has led diversity, equity, and inclusion presentations for CEOs of major corporations in an effort to increase minority participation at all levels. For decades, Dr. Murillo has led by example. In 2020, she was named as one of the "Most Admired CEOs in Houston" by the Houston Business Journal and as one of the "Top CEOs in Texas" by Texas CEO Magazine for her outstanding leadership. Dr. Murillo's story is inspiring and serves as an example for others to follow and be able to reach their full potential."

Mayor Sylvester Turner
Houston, Texas

"As the Founding Executive Producer and Host on six Audacy radio stations, CBS KHOU 11 television, Univision television, and radio simultaneously, Dr. Laura Murillo's capacity to serve as an influencer at all levels shines through. CEOs and executives seek her guidance in the new era of diversity, equity, and inclusion.

She has been named the 2021 Global Leader of Influence Honoree by the World Affairs Council and is among the most influential and powerful women in Texas. She was also acknowledged as one of the Women Who Run Houston by the *Houston Chronicle*, Mother of the Year by the *Houston Latin Philharmonic*, The Top Latino Leader Award by the National Diversity Council, G7 Global Impact Honoree, TWEF International Leadership Award, *Global Influence Magazine's* Championing the Success of Women in the Workplace, to name a few.

All of these accomplishments are a testament to her tenacity and ability to bring people together."

Sarah Frazier
Sr. Vice President and Market Manager, Audacy

FOREWORD

I have shared in life's journey with Dr. Laura Murillo for close to two decades. We have experienced the human condition, with all of its trials and tribulations, and have been blessed to share many personal and professional successes.

Laura is a brilliant and fearless traveler who has broken glass ceilings on her journey as a leader, community advocate, educator, and mother, and she has brought many along with her. Consistent with her writings, Laura's life demonstrates how a leader can remain compassionate and attuned to the needs of others through adversity. She shows leaders how to maintain a sense of urgency and anticipate what is needed at the national, community, and personal levels.

Her leadership of one of the most influential Hispanic Chamber of Commerce in the country, demonstrates the spirit of economic cooperation and civility that is so critical in business and society, in good times and particularly during times of difficulty and uncertainty. Nothing better exemplified what is required of leaders than the global COVID pandemic. During this complex time of unpredictability, human beings showed that we will rise to the occasion with bravery, adeptness, and altruism. Laura shined her bright light by inspiring others to action and leveraging the natural inclination of those around her. No matter the circumstance, for Laura, the impossible is always possible.

Throughout her career, she has helped young people build maps that outlay generous plans, not only for themselves, but also for their communities and our world. Her own map, and the maps of those she influences, lay the foundation to imagine new possibilities and expectations for humanity.

In this book, Laura offers something of extraordinary value. She recounts what she has learned through areas many are only beginning to understand on the horizon of social change, transformational leadership, and service. Through her travels in all these realms, she has learned to move past adversity and bring vitality to all areas of life.

The optimism required to execute Laura's work is often idealistic. However, Laura is not naive. Even when leaders are at our best, there are obstacles. She suggests that being a good leader is complex, it takes effort and persistence, and it requires a holistic perspective which includes plans for failure, the anticipation of barriers, and a reserve for the events of life that just happen.

Laura delineates a way through life's professional journey that acknowledges the complexities associated with being a leader and celebrates the value of helping others be more effective on their own leadership journey.

Her journey and accomplishments are certainly worthy of our appreciation.

Dr. Heather Kopecky
Senior Partner and Executive Coach, Korn Ferry International

TABLE OF CONTENTS

CHOICES 1

    HUMBLE BEGINNINGS 6

THREE PS TO MY SUCCESS 15

    PEOPLE 17
    PASSION 21
    PERSISTENCE 27

BE BOLD, BE STRONG 35

    TAKE CARE OF THE JOB YOU HAVE AND THE NEXT ONE WILL FIND YOU 41
    INVEST IN YOURSELF 43
    REACH YOUR FULL POTENTIAL 48
    SAY YOU ARE AND YOU SHALL BECOME 55

GALLERY 61

WORK WITH URGENCY 103

    THE WAY YOU DO ANYTHING IS THE WAY YOU DO EVERYTHING 104
    THE NEW ERA OF DEI 105
    LEAD 109
    DIVERSITY CHAMPIONS 114
    BECOME A CONNECTOR 130
    DEI: MAKE IT MATTER 132
    SERVANT LEADERSHIP 135

INTUITION 139

    A MOTHER'S LOVE 140
    BLINK 147
    PITCH FROM THE MOUND 149
    BE READY AND STAY READY 153
    OWN YOUR SEAT AT THE TABLE 158

MY HOUR OF INSPIRATION 163

ABOUT THE AUTHOR 169

CHAPTER 1

CHOICES

H e came from nowhere. My mom and I were running errands for the day and had just finished exchanging some items at Gulfgate Mall on a beautiful, sunny Saturday morning. There was nothing unusual about the day, except a feeling in my gut. As we pulled into the parking spot, I noticed to the left and front of the spot there were bushes, small shrubs—no big deal. Yet, something inside me whispered, "Don't park there." I didn't pay much attention to the voice. After all, we were just running in to return a few things, and then we would be out and on our way. Not listening to my intuition that day ultimately changed my entire life.

At eighteen years old and fresh out of high school, I had the world in the palm of my hand. I felt invincible and I believed I could succeed at just about anything I set my mind to. I had developed an unshakable focus and a dogged work ethic while working at my dad's neighborhood restaurant from the time I was ten years old. I started out just piddling around, waiting tables and helping in the kitchen. Over time, I took on new responsibilities, like greeting customers, cashing out the register at the end of the day, and ordering supplies, all the necessary tasks of running a family business. By engaging with the employees, I was able to speak a lot of Spanish and appreciate the hard work they did every day to feed their families. As the youngest of nine, I was the one who tagged along with my dad to the restaurant. I felt a deep connection to both of my parents and was honored to have a solid relationship with both of them.

With our errands complete, and back at the car, I slid into the driver's seat of my shiny red 1985 Ford Thunderbird, a graduation gift from my dad. As soon as my mom opened the passenger-side door and eased down into the seat, a man appeared on her side, startling us both. He pushed her into the seat, reached across her body, and aimed his gun just inches from my head. His voice was rough with anger, his breathing quick with the urgency to get what he had come for, whatever that was.

"Get out of the car now!" He said. "Leave everything. Get out now."

"No, no, no!" my mom screamed, shaking uncontrollably, unable to move from her seat.

With a quick glance at the perpetrator, I took stock of him. He was about twenty years old, slender, and tall, wearing a green T-shirt and blue jeans. Somehow, I managed to remain calm, almost too calm. "Take what you want," I said. "Just let us get out of the car."

As he pressed the gun into my right temple, his hand shook, and I could feel the vibration of his nervous grip on the handle with his finger on the trigger. When I didn't move, he pressed the barrel even further against my flesh. I turned my head slightly towards him and looked deep into his eyes, searching for an indication that there was at least an ounce of reason within him, something that would ignite the compassion to spare my mom and me from any further trauma. Instead, all I saw in his eyes was desperation and anger. With my mom still screaming and nearly hyperventilating, a frightening thought crossed my mind. *Oh my God, he's going to kill me in front of my mother, and he's going to kill her too.* Despite the urgency of the moment, I felt terrible that she would have to witness such a scene. No parent should ever have to experience that kind of tragedy.

"Get out!" the gunman shouted, louder this time, with more anger and desperation and the gun firmly against my head. "I'm not playing with you."

Then came the sound, like an echo in a dark room, bouncing off cement walls. *Click!* He pulled the trigger and, with that simple act, had the power to destroy my life. My eyes shut tightly and my shoulders raised to my ears in tense anticipation, ready to feel the pain of the bullet entering my head and exploding. In a millisecond, I envisioned the horror of remnants of my brain tissue splattered throughout the vehicle, covering my mom, the car seats, the windshield. Yet, that simple click yielded nothing. The gun had jammed. With uncontrollably shaking hands, I quickly grabbed the driver's side door handle and pushed the door open.

"Mommy!" I yelled. She was frozen with fear, unable to exit on the passenger side, where the gunman leaned across her body. With little thought, I took hold of her hand and snatched her petite body across the center console and out my door, her shoes still on the floor where her feet had been. In what seemed like one swift movement, the gunman hopped into the passenger seat, slid over to the driver's side, and drove off, leaving my mom and me standing in the parking lot of Gulfgate Mall, shaking and in shock. I watched the car speed away, the strap of my mom's purse dangling out the passenger door. Relieved that we were still alive, I stood there, holding my mom tightly, and we cried.

In the days that followed, I was terrified that the gunman would find us and try to kill us. He had driven off with not only my car, but also with our purses, which included all our identification. My mind went wild, thinking of all the things he could do with that information. To help ease my concerns, my dad changed the locks on every door in our house. We canceled our credit cards and got new ones. I got a new driver's license and replaced all the other items that were stolen. Still, I was in a state of panic, afraid to leave the house and afraid to be there. I felt like a prisoner in my own home. My mind created scenarios of the gunman regretting that he didn't shoot us and coming after us to finish the job. There I was, eighteen years old, having been held at gunpoint, and I was a total wreck. My life had been spared and it was just beginning, but I was afraid to live it.

———————— ● ————————

College was next in my future, and I knew the transition would bring a very different experience from my years at Austin High School, where my classmates voted me Most Likely to Succeed, Most Popular, and Class President, and where I graduated with honors among the top five percent of my peers. Austin High School is in the Houston Independent School District located in Houston's East End.

By the time I entered college, I was working three jobs—at the family restaurant, at my sister Lupe's beauty salon, and at a radio station. I didn't know what I wanted to do when I grew up, but I loved helping people and I thought being a journalist, in some capacity, would be important because I saw so few people in that space who looked liked me. With so much on my plate, I buried my emotions about the car-jacking and didn't tell anyone about the emotional turmoil I was experiencing, partly because I didn't want anyone to pity me and also because I didn't want to feel like a victim. I was losing days and weeks, focused on what could have been instead of being grateful for what was. In short, I was living in fear.

Even more than the fear, I felt a grave sense of guilt for having put my mom in harm's way. I blamed myself for not trusting my intuition that told me not to park in the spot. My poor decision could have ended both our lives. I was overwhelmed with guilt that I had endangered my mother's life. Interestingly, my mother's response was to panic at the moment of the attack, but following the incident, she was surprisingly calm and thankful to God that nothing happened to either of us. Our responses were so different, and whether I realized it or not, I learned by watching how my mother responded to the event. She was resilient and she quickly moved on, even though I still suffered from the trauma.

Thankfully, about three weeks later, the police arrested the gunman and found he was tied to a string of similar crimes in other states. That didn't do much to ease my mind. I was still traumatized by the incident, and I worried I would never be able to function normally. Everything startled me. I knew my fears were unfounded since the gunman had been caught, but fear had carved out a place in my mind that caused me to isolate myself from the world, from my life.

One day, while at home alone, I began saying aloud to myself, "Mom's okay, you're okay. Everything is going to be okay." I paced the floor of my bedroom, ringing my hands and staring at my feet as I placed one foot in front of the other. "Mom survived. You survived. You are here, now, and you have to live." It was as if someone outside of me was giving a pep-talk, hoping to snap me out of a darkness that threatened my existence. I was a young woman with a future, but I had allowed a terrible experience to paralyze me with fear. I knew I couldn't go on living like that. I realized then that I wanted more. I wanted to live. That strong desire ignited in me a resiliency I didn't know was there. I realized I had a choice. I could either let that one person, that one incident, control and overpower me, or I could use that experience to my benefit, as an opportunity to strengthen myself. I chose life and made a conscious decision to live every moment with urgency, to be joyful, more appreciative, more thoughtful, and more engaged with each person in my life. An incredible zest for life was created, and I willingly embraced it.

My decision to release the fear and instead embrace the power to control my thoughts and actions felt wonderful. Somewhere deep inside, a determination grew that would not allow one person to keep me from being the best I could be. Instead, I realized how fortunate I was to survive being held at gunpoint and that I would not let my life be in vain. Despite how traumatic that event had been, neither my mom nor I had been physically hurt, and I was grateful for that. In fact, the incident made us even closer than we had been. It was a strange, terrible experience only the two of us shared. Yet, I had to choose how I would live with it. I chose to acknowledge that everything was okay, that I was resilient, and that I would persist in every endeavor going forward.

I transitioned from fear, guilt, and grief to joy, happiness, and a zest for life. My appreciation for life grew daily, and I became obsessed with living my life to the fullest. My focus turned to accomplishing as much as I could. I decided that whatever I put in my mind to do, I would do it and take nothing for granted. From then on, I committed to live every moment with urgency and passion. That single decision was a pivotal choice point in my life, allowing me to see the power and impact of my resiliency and the value of taking these lessons from life experiences and moving forward with people, passion, and persistence.

Humble Beginnings

Braving the Rio Grande River, my parents emigrated from Mexico to the U.S. as teenagers. Married and in search of a brighter future than their parents had, they arrived together with dreams of starting a family, building a business, and living the American dream. They couldn't have known the journey they would take to accomplish those dreams or that the youngest of their nine children would credit their influence as the motivation for her own success.

All of four foot six, my mother, Tomasa González, was a small woman with a big heart. How she managed to raise nine children (my brother, Armando, died in his infancy), while her husband worked as a tile mason, still baffles me. She spoke very little English, so when she spoke to her children in Spanish, we listened. She was stern, yet loving toward us and compassionate and caring to everyone she encountered.

A beautiful woman with fair skin and hazel eyes, she was the heart of our family and was cherished by those who knew her. She taught me what it means to be compassionate and to be a servant leader. Her lessons have guided me throughout my education, my career, and especially my life as a mother. Through many situations in life, I could hear her voice directing me, whether I was a subordinate or in a leadership position. All in all, my mom's tender spirit has played out in me through all aspects of my life. Her hobby was gardening. In many ways she planted seeds of love and wisdom that would bloom later in my life.

Mom always worried that I was working and studying too hard. She valued my ambitious nature, and knew my schooling was important, but she felt I needed to take a break from the seemingly never-ending to-

dos I imposed on myself. With each degree I e⸱
for another one. She would say, "Oh, my gos
about you. You keep studying, but every time
you have another exam or degree to study for. I
Maybe you need to find a new job because the⸳
to school."

and come h
purchase
Park r
vet

All I could do was appreciate her deep love
that love in many ways, one of which was to leav⸵
would cut a single rose from her garden, put it in ⸱ ⸱⸱⸱⸱ crystal flower
vase, and place it on the desk whenever I studied. That was her way of
supporting me. It was sweet and simple and sincere. When I finally
crossed the stage with my doctorate in hand, Mia in my arms, and Marisa
by my side, my mom said, "I am so proud of you. You're a great mom,
a great daughter. I'm so thankful you have reached all your dreams. Even
though I thought it was too much for you to be a mom, go to school
full time, and work full time, you did it!" Those words meant the world
to me.

My father, Jose González, was the yang to my mother's calm and
compassionate yin. If she was my heart, he was my inspiration to work
hard, overcome obstacles, and live with urgency. Six foot four, tall, dark,
and handsome, he was a confident man whose presence was undeniable.
When he walked into a room, people would say, "Who is that?" He
exuded his charisma and self-assurance in a way that not only attracted
attention, but also welcomed engagement. He had a powerful, strong
voice and connected authentically with people, greeting each one with
his eyes so focused that whoever he was speaking with probably felt they
were the only one in the room with him.

Despite my parents' limited education, my father taught himself to
read and write English, a testament to his desire to succeed in this
country where he had chosen to raise his family. He had a strong work
ethic and always put in long hours of sometimes back-breaking labor.
Working as a tile mason for many years, he learned the craft so well that
he ultimately opened a warehouse of his own near our home. Dad was
a competitor, a persistent go-getter who knew he had to work harder
than the next guy to get ahead. He had always aspired to be an
entrepreneur, and he demonstrated to his family the value of owning a
business.

As the youngest of nine, I saw him go to work early in the morning

ome late at night, eventually selling his tile business to
a Mexican restaurant called El Jardin in Houston's Magnolia
neighborhood, along with my mother; my brother Joe, a Vietnam
veteran; and Joe's wife, Alma. Armed with an entrepreneurial spirit,
working indoors and owning his business after many years of manual
labor became a labor of love. After forty years, that restaurant remains
in the family.

Whenever he went to the restaurant or to meet with vendors, my
father presented the image of success. He took great pride in dressing
well, and I enjoyed seeing him clad in his best attire, so much so that I
would lay out his clothes the night before. "What am I wearing
tomorrow, Laura?" He would ask. I laid out his shoes, shirt, and pants
for him, alongside his gold Presidential Rolex watch, which he adored.

My father and brother Arthur building my dad's
tile business in our childhood neighborhood
located in Houston's East End, Magnolia Park.

Well-groomed from head to toe, he didn't have to speak when he arrived. He just walked into a room and commanded the presence of everyone there. Strong enough to use his body language, yet aware enough to not be boisterous, people automatically knew he was the man in charge.

By the time I started working at our family's restaurant with my father and Big Brother Joe, I was ten years old, and I loved every moment of it. All my other siblings, except my brother Daniel, were married and on their own. I cleaned tables, swept the floor, and even ran errands with my dad before finally moving up to become a hostess and work the cash register. One of my favorite jobs was working the window when orders came in. I loved being the quality control person, although the job didn't carry that title back then. I made sure everything was up to par and looked the way it was supposed to look to ensure a satisfied customer. No job was too small for me.

"Go pick up trash in the parking lot" meant "Don't pick up some of it; pick up all of it," and I did. I wanted to be the best at doing whatever my dad asked of me because he instilled in me that every job is important, no matter how small. Truth be told, I enjoyed the fast pace of the restaurant business. With a full house during my shifts, I gained an appreciation for multi-tasking and for paying attention to detail.

While I loved the organized chaos, I also loved the opportunity to be with my father and to work with him for hours on end. In years prior, he'd worked long, hard days, so by the time he got home late at night, I was already asleep. Because of that, I didn't have the quality time with him that I craved. Working alongside him at the restaurant satisfied my desire to be with him. We enjoyed so many simple yet precious moments together, like sitting at our favorite table, where we would eat a quick lunch and listen as the juke box blared Mexican tunes. The only English-language song on the playlist was by Elton John and Kiki Dee, "Don't Go Breaking My Heart" and we both loved it. I think of my dad when I hear that song. I took advantage of those special times with my father to observe all the traits that made him who he was: charming, hardworking, competitive, and smart. The twelve years I worked at the restaurant were some of the most formative and memorable of my life.

My dad had a great personality. He was very charismatic and was also quite the prankster. For my sixteenth birthday, he gave me a gift that was unusual, to say the least.

"Here's your gift, Laura. Happy birthday," he said, handing me an old cardboard box. He had filled it with trash and rotten food and placed it on the table where he and I would have quick meals between work. It wreaked with the stench of rotten food.

With my nose upturned at both the smell and the presentation of the gift, I proceeded to open it, hoping there was something of value inside. I opened the box and sifted through the dirty mess until I finally reached the bottom. There, I found a rectangular box. I looked up at my dad and saw his smile. Within the box was a gold bracelet with sixteen diamonds, one for each year of my life. He didn't need to explain the lesson he had just taught me. I already knew what he was communicating to me. Sometimes you have to sift through the mess to get to the reward. Attaining the end goal sometimes requires you to see something not as it is, but as you visualize it to be. This is one way to attain great outcomes even in the midst of seemingly dire situations.

Observing my dad during his business dealings—whether negotiating, networking, or simply managing the day-to-day operations of the business—was the best on-the-job training I could ever receive. He instilled in me his realization that we have a chance in this country and that every experience is an opportunity that must be acted upon. We choose, moment by moment, to either sit back and observe or to act. He was a take-action kind of person, and I admired that about him.

One of the things that amused me most about my dad's impact on others is that, at times, he could be viewed as intimidating. Whether because of his stature, his booming voice, or his confident personality, some people who engaged with him cowered beneath his domineering persona. My experience with him was quite different. I was never intimidated by my father. He told me that, even at age ten, I wasn't afraid of him. Little did I know having that kind of relationship with him prepared me to engage with strong, assertive men in male-dominated settings without feeling intimidated or overwhelmed. Thanks to my dad, I am strong enough to handle myself in a room full of powerful men.

There are so many characteristics I have taken from both my parents as a roadmap to follow: serving others, working hard, being diligent, and finding a way to overcome challenges. As I grew into adulthood and began to develop my authentic persona, I consciously took what I saw as the best qualities from my father and the best qualities from my mother and utilized them to make me the best I could be.

When my father passed away at age sixty-three, I was twenty-four years old. He had suffered several health challenges and had been hospitalized many times. When I visited with him one time at the hospital, he said, "When I die, I hope you guys don't close the restaurant the day of my funeral." I was speechless. Even on his deathbed, he was thinking about the business. That's how focused and dedicated he was. We talked more that afternoon, and he said, "You're going to do big things, Laura. You will leave a great legacy." At first, I wasn't sure what he was communicating to me, but he was sincere, so I listened intently. I instinctively wanted to do well for him because he expected it from me. From my vantage point, he had done big things in his life, and yet he thought I would do bigger things because of my education.

By then, his larger-than-life frame had dwindled to just over one hundred pounds, and he had a steel halo screwed into his head as a result of many illnesses. It broke my heart to see him suffering and I wanted him to be out of his misery. As I sat with him in the hospital, I recalled something he used to say to me when I was a little girl: "When you get married, you're going to break my heart." I never understood how he could expect that something as joyous as his youngest child getting married would break his heart. Little did I know the power of his words as a foreshadowing of his death. Six months after I got married, he died in the hospital with his family by his side.

The experiences of my formative years have shaped me into who I am and let me know I have choices. The long-term impact of nearly losing my life at a young age provided me with an appreciation and gratitude for life itself and an understanding that time is my most precious commodity. Because of my early experiences, I learned I have choices. I can either work with urgency or I can let tragedies slow me down. I can compartmentalize things, and do the most in the least amount of time, still getting the results I hope for with the help of others, or I can sit on the sidelines and wait for something to happen. I can choose to control the things I can control and not waste time on things I cannot control. I always have a choice.

When I am faced with a challenge, I think about the obstacles my parents overcame when they made the choice to cross the Rio Grande and come to the U.S., and I ask myself, "Is this really an obstacle? What are my choices in this situation?" Every time, I conclude that what seems like an obstacle really isn't. I have choices in how I will approach difficulties. I owe it to my parents to achieve my goals. Serving others is my way of giving thanks to God for saving my life.

I demonstrate my appreciation for life by doing things that matter in my personal life and in my career. Today, as President and CEO of the award-winning Houston Hispanic Chamber of Commerce, I have the privilege of waking up every day and working alongside an incredible board and amazing staff who have led us to becoming one of the most influential chambers in the nation as we serve our community. In 2007, when I was recruited for my position, I visualized the Chamber for what it could be and not for what it was. I knew that recruiting the right board and staff would help us live up to our tagline, "The Leader of Houston's New Majority" and usher in this new era of diversity, equity, and inclusion.

LEAD IN LIFE MOMENT

The Lead in Life Moments in this book are for the young leaders out there. They are lessons I have learned on my journey to Lead in Life. Apply them with passion and persistence and watch how your actions inspire the people in your life.

As an advocate and a take-action kind of person, like my dad, I have an undeniable passion for life that stands as the foundation for my personal and professional brand. As a high-energy, results-focused change agent, I have developed the persistence to do anything I set my mind to, and to do it with urgency because I know tomorrow is not promised.

From age ten until I graduated from college, I worked alongside my father at the family business, El Jardin Restaurant.

CHAPTER 2

THREE Ps TO MY SUCCESS

W ith the click of a desperate man's gun, all my tomorrows could have vanished. But that was not the plan for my life. Because of that experience and so many others, my mind is wired for appreciation, not for negativity. No longer does fear fill my life. Instead, my every thought and action is fueled by people, passion, and persistence.

Not one of my accomplishments has been achieved alone. Surrounding myself with people who believe in me and who value the knowledge and experience I offer has been the catalyst to propel me from one success to the next. Whether a mentor who guided me to apply for my doctorate, a sponsor who believed in my ideas enough to fund them, a media executive who saw promise in my message, an organization that valued my experience, or a community that appreciated my authenticity, people have always been at the core of my success.

The support of the people in my life has allowed me to live life with passion. My passionate pursuit of goals in service to others is the secret ingredient to my ability to accomplish practically anything I set my mind to. Passion, for me, is the ardent enthusiasm at the core of each undertaking. From the very first nudges to accomplish a goal, I search my heart and soul for that spark of passion that lets me know to continue taking one step after the other with urgency until the thing is accomplished.

Through uphill battles, easy-going sprints, and surprises that reveal valuable lessons, persistence gets me to the finish line. Tenacity and perseverance are natural traits for me. From the time I was a child, I have had a built-in "no-quit" mode that won't allow me to stop until a job is finished, no matter the struggles, setbacks, resistance, refusals, distractions, or delays. In every pursuit, I persist through difficulties, knowing that if my ultimate goal seems distant or impossible, I will find a way, I will try something else, I will ask for help, I will figure it out. Nothing is insurmountable when my three Ps—people, passion, and persistence—are activated.

I use these three Ps to help me navigate through the day, through every project and goal, and to stay focused on the details on the journey, rather than be overwhelmed by the whole. Like putting together a five-thousand-piece puzzle, determining how and where to begin can sometimes be confusing. I assemble the pieces as best I can, then I bring in others who might see the big picture in a different light. They add value and perspective, a diversity of thought and opinion. By then, I start to develop a passion for seeing the end game. Quitting is not an option for me, and that is why my persistence kicks in. That passion drives my persistence to finish the puzzle by turning on my three Ps to success—people, passion, and persistence—and working with urgency to complete it so I can begin another one.

People are like the five thousand pieces that comprise the entire puzzle, turning an idea into something we can all be a part of. Passion is my love for what I do, including the joy of sharing the journey and the outcome with others. Persistence is never quitting, no matter the obstacle. All the while, I find ways to make it a pleasurable experience for myself and for others, to learn from those who have contributed, and to see that without the diversity of experiences, if I worked alone, the puzzle would not be the same beautiful tapestry.

People

My dad used to tell me to surround myself with two types of people: those who are smarter than I am, to advance my education and career, and those I can serve and for whom I can be an inspiration by sharing my gifts, talents, and insights. That advice has served me well. I am who I am partly because of the people I've surrounded myself with. Thanks again to my dad, the intimidation factor regarding those with strong personalities just isn't there for me. Instead, I am intrigued by them, and I want to get closer to them to learn as much as I can, the same as it was for my dad and me. I suppose I am drawn to strong personalities like a moth to a flame.

As I learn and watch the people I engage with in business, I pick up habits and traits that make me better. They serve as an inspiration to me, especially at times when I feel overwhelmed with all I have to do. At those times, I often reach out to one of my mentors, either for lunch or through a simple phone call. The casual conversation soon becomes a session in which we share insights and possibilities. By the time we finish talking, I feel much better. I realize that, in fact, I am not doing too much, especially compared to them. Instead, I am doing exactly what I need to do to further my goals and aspirations.

My mentors multiply my efforts in service to my goals and reassure me that I am on the right track. That inspires me to keep going. Like them, I thrive in the fast lane. It is a pace I have chosen because my life experiences have influenced my productivity and my desire to contribute to society. Investing my time in building relationships with people who add value to my life is similar to running a race. To be my best, I always want to run with those who help me run faster, those who are experienced runners and know what winning feels like, those who run with me and encourage me along the way, and those who push me to the finish line because, as leaders, they know my success is their success. This is how I learn things, improve, and elevate my game. Just as important to me is passing on and sharing lessons to help others run their race and reach their full potential.

LEAD IN LIFE MOMENT

Surrounding yourself with motivators and high achievers who help you feel valuable, important, and respected is a critical aspect of success.

———————— ● ————————

Before she was even a year old, my elder daughter, Marisa, had the aptitude for knowing how things are put together. She would line up her blocks on the floor in a definite pattern—red, blue, red, blue—something that was a higher-level skillset for a child that age. By the time she reached second grade, it was evident that she loved science. As a parent, I nurtured that ability. When she developed an interest in knitting, I offered to send her to a class to learn how to do it right, but she refused. She wanted to learn by doing. One stitch after another, Marisa taught herself to knit, weaving the needle in and through the strands of yarn to create beautiful patterns. She was relentless and taught herself to knit not only accurately, but also quickly. What she didn't realize at the time was that she was strengthening her beautiful hands with each turn of the needle. In essence, she was building and creating on her own.

By the time she reached ninth grade, Marisa already knew she wanted to be an engineer. In her freshman year at St. John's School, an elite, top-ranked Texas private school, located in the River Oaks neighborhood of Houston, she joined an engineering club that was slated to participate in the Shell Oil Company's Mechanical Engineering Eco Marathon, an international competition in which students build an actual car. As one of only two girls, the only Latina, and the youngest member of the team, she faced a lot of hurdles. The boys on the team tried to relegate her to menial tasks, like designing the team T-shirt, but she refused. With her insistence on doing the real work involved in the project, Marisa and her team soon learned the value of the unique ability she had developed as a young girl.

When the time came to saw the heavy steel metal frame to build the car, all the boys tried to saw the pieces of the frame, but could not. Marisa insisted on trying her hand at it, but the boys refused to let her try. Finally, one senior boy said, "Let Marisa try." Reluctantly, her teammates agreed. Like a pro, Marisa picked up the hand saw and cut through the metal on the first try. She went on to cut every piece for the entire car frame, a skill that required both strength and precision.

LEAD IN LIFE MOMENT

When you know you're good at something, don't just sit back and accept the role others offer you. Know your worth and what you are capable of. Advocate for yourself, and if you're in a position to do so, advocate for others.

Ultimately, her team competed in the international competition. What she didn't know—couldn't have known—was that her ability to knit would come in handy (pun intended) in her engineering pursuits. Marisa became the leader of the St. John's School Engineering Club in her senior year, the first Latina in the school's history to do so. She went on to the Ivy League, where she earned a degree in mechanical engineering from the number-one ranked engineering program in the country at Columbia University, in New York City, in 2021, and today, she is employed as an astrophysics researcher in the Schiminovich Astrophysical Instrumentation Laboratory in New York City.

As a leader, it is important to know that people within your organization have skills and talents. Learn to cultivate and develop those individuals as part of your strategy for diversity, equity, and inclusion (DEI). When you hire for knowledge, ability, and passion, you can trust that you've done your part. From there, recognize that everyone brings something of value to the table and should have an equitable chance at opportunity. This doesn't mean someone else with equal skill or ability has to lose. What it means is that when the playing field is fair and open to all, when each person is allowed to demonstrate their gifts and strengths for the betterment of the whole, the entire organization can benefit.

In order to embrace the new era of equity, fairness, and impartiality, organizations must examine long-held beliefs that have morphed into discriminatory practices. Change the way you look at your team members and you'll be surprised at how much value they bring to the table.

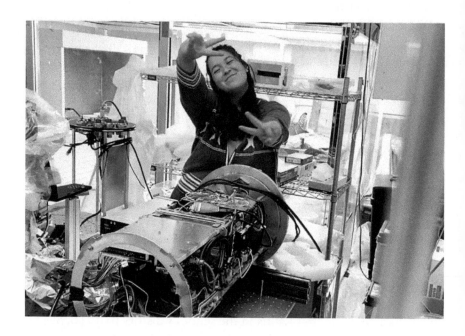

My daughter, Marisa is an Astrophysics Researcher in the Schiminovich Astrophysical Instrumentation Laboratory where she works on the Circumgalactic H-Alpha Spectograph in New York City.

*With my daughters, Marisa (l) and Mia (r) at Marisa's 2021
graduation from the Ivy Leagues' Columbia University in New
York City, where she earned a mechanical engineering degree from
the number one ranked program in the country.*

Passion

If you're going to be a good leader, you have to feel passionate about
what you do. Passion wakes you up early in the morning and keeps you
going for the long haul. For some, passion is a choice. For me, it is an
innate drive that plays out in everything I do. Passion is the energy force
that allows my mind to be creative first thing in the morning and pushes
me to keep going well into the night, until my work is done.

Whether I am speaking before a group of global leaders, discussing
economic development opportunities, attending an event, spending time
with my daughters, or just sitting still and enjoying the beauty of nature,
I do it with passion. My passion for my work, and for life in general,
comes from my sincere appreciation for the blessings that have been

bestowed upon me. The fact that my parents came here with nothing and were able to create a family and devote their lives to our success is more than admirable. My mother dedicated her life to her children. My father, whether he realized it or not, set an example of a strong work ethic. Their spirits reside in me, and I see them show up time and again in my dedication to my daughters' success and in my deep passion for my work.

———————— ● ————————

Even in times of adversity, my passion allows me to see the bright light at the end of an otherwise very dark tunnel. In 2015, I decided to become a single parent after twenty-four years of marriage. I began a new chapter in my life when both girls were admitted into St. Johns School. We left the suburbs and moved just blocks away from their new school.

In March of 2020, it seemed as if the whole world came to a screeching halt. The greatest losses were the more than three million lives prematurely ended due to the COVID-19 virus. To say the pandemic overwhelmed the world would be an understatement. For those who were fortunate to work remotely, the global shut-down was an opportunity to pivot, to figure out life in a new way, to innovate, and to progress into the future with a fresh perspective. Despite the devastation experienced by so many in 2020, including me, the shelter-in-place ordinance allowed me the opportunity to think deeply about what I wanted and how my passion for life could ignite ideas and desires that had been simmering within me for years.

My primary outlet for exhibiting my passion is direct engagement with people, but I didn't have that due to COVID restrictions. What I did have was my girls at home with me, something that wouldn't have been otherwise. Marisa had to leave Columbia University in New York and spend more than a year at home while keeping up with her studies. Mia didn't get her once-in-a-lifetime opportunity to be a first-year student enjoying the beautiful campus of Georgetown University, in Washington, DC, named among the best universities in the world for studying government and international relations. Instead, she was relegated to study and attend virtual courses from our home. There were certainly worse places to study, and my gratitude overflowed, knowing that the three of us had this beautiful space to live out our pandemic experience. In the midst of the COVID isolation, I was humbled by appreciating the many blessings of my life.

Meanwhile, as the founding executive producer and host of the Chamber's CBS and Univision TV and radio programs, I continued recording from my living room and had strategic calls from sunup to sundown. Like everyone, I had the choice to view the situation as a horrible experience or as a blessing. I chose the latter. I was grateful the girls and I could be together for more than a year and that we made time to interact in ways we wouldn't have otherwise.

During the first few weeks of the shelter-in-place ordinance issued by the Texas governor in response to COVID, I was worried about people dying and losing their jobs, families being displaced from their homes, and children becoming separated from an education system that had not figured out the best way to educate students remotely. I secured interviews with four school superintendents from across our region and allowed families to ask questions over the air. Immediately, I went into action mode, searching for ways to provide solutions and to help in any way I could. No one knew what the next best step was to help those in need, so I asked myself, "What can I do with the information and resources I have?" My answer came simply by evaluating my natural passion for helping people.

As CEO of the Houston Hispanic Chamber of Commerce, my day-to-day work, which involved going from one meeting or event to the next, from one end of town to the other, was flipped upside down. Due to COVID restrictions, I was not driving across town to secure funding for a program or speak to a group. Eliminating the commute meant I had to work in a new way, and I went after it aggressively. In turbo mode, I began to aggregate the resources at my disposal. The obvious first step was to find a way to use the media platform I had developed years earlier to serve others by helping them meet their immediate needs.

I was able to capitalize on the platform to reach an audience of more than three million on six stations of CBS Radio (later renamed Audacy), CBS KHOU-11 television, and Univision television and radio in Spanish. My goal was to establish an ambitious media platform that would set us apart from other organizations. This was something that had never been done at any chamber in the country, and we were doing it during the pandemic. Not only was I interviewing people for the TV and radio show, but I was also being interviewed nationally and internationally about the economic impact of COVID, vaccination information, and disparities between essential and nonessential workers, all critical information people needed to look forward to the future.

Without a doubt, we demonstrated that the Chamber was part of the mainstream population and that we had a reach and influence not only in the Hispanic community, but also throughout the entire city of Houston. My objective was to use that platform to connect those in need with those who could help, no matter their cultural or ethnic background, using my connections with corporate partners to assist small businesses in securing loans, help families extend leases on their housing and secure needed food, and support students with educational resources. Before I knew it, I was being featured on virtual town hall meetings with the governor, providing resources and information to the greater Houston population.

My messages explored innovative ways to address the challenges and the needs of so many entrepreneurs, business leaders, families, and young people in the city of Houston. I collaborated with organizations like the Workforce Commission, the U.S. Small Business Administration, the White House Administration, the Federal Reserve, Texas Medical Center, Harris County, the City of Houston, experts, and elected officials who could provide advice and guidance remotely to business owners and the greater Houston region. My passion for helping people caused me to ask critical questions that would connect people with jobs and other resources to support them during such a difficult time. Those connections supported the supply chain of the city to help keep it moving.

As a result of our efforts, the Houston Hispanic Chamber of Commerce earned two awards—Outstanding Diversity Organization and the Helping Hand Award—from the *Houston Business Journal*. Admission into the Harvard University Women on Corporate Boards executive program enabled me to join a cohort of women from across the globe who have accomplished extraordinary things, including serving on multiple boards. Poised to be the next leaders in corporate, political, and government sectors, these women offered their expert advice on being productive in a career and being prepared to serve others and lead in life. My passion was also acknowledged by *Global Influence Magazine* when I was recognized as a "Champion for the Success of Women in the Workplace" and the World Affairs Council named me the "2021 Global Leader of Influence Honoree".

As COVID continued to devastate the U.S. and the world, people developed ways to manage the diminished travel and, for some, the new work-from-home reality. I was asked to submit my name for a three-year term on the Federal Reserve Board's Community Advisory Council (CAC) in Washington, DC, which was a long shot because only ten people from across the country serve on this committee. To my surprise, I received a phone call from Daron Peschel, Vice President of the Dallas Federal Reserve, that I had been selected as the first Houstonian to serve on the CAC. The position is a national voice for Houston, and the work influences monetary policy, housing, unemployment, inflation, homelessness, and other areas with a direct impact on regional and national policy.

In a virtual meeting with Federal Reserve Chairman Jerome Powell, the CAC discussed recommendations he could share with Congress, and I was honored to provide my knowledge, advice, and recommendations on relevant policy matters and emerging issues and to share the stories and anecdotes of Houstonians. Furthering my drive to increase my footprint on the business landscape, *Texas CEO Magazine* named me among the top CEOs in Texas, alongside Dallas Mavericks owner Mark Cuban, Marc Boom, CEO of Houston Methodist Hospital, and others for our outstanding leadership in the midst of the COVID pandemic.

Although 2020 was one of my most productive years professionally, personally it was one of the worst years of my life. My eldest brother, Joe, died at the age of 69. Losing him was devastating and overwhelming for me. He was fifteen years my senior. I called him Big Brother Joe, and from the time my dad passed away, he became my father figure. I was heartbroken over his death, and the only way I knew to deal with it was to channel my grief into doing something I had talked to him about doing for years.

Given the stay-at-home protocol, I was no longer attending multiple events each night and on weekends. Still, the virtual calls continued, beginning early in the morning and ending late at night and even over weekends. Despite that, there was no better time for me to write this book than during the global pandemic. As I developed the framework for my message, I sat on our balcony on the 27th floor, at our penthouse. I enjoyed doing the work I was so passionate about, considering my blessings and the gratitude I had for being able to help others in my life. At a time when the world was shut down, I drew upon my passion for my work, and I tried to demonstrate to my daughters the resilience I learned from my parents.

As I grieved my brother's death, I was so grateful to have both Marisa and Mia at home with me for over a year when they would otherwise have been in college. I watched them work, hour after hour, on virtual classes. I saw my elder daughter, Marisa, taking thermodynamics and astrophysics courses and manipulating all types of machinery and gadgets to complete her engineering projects. My younger daughter, Mia, wrote paper after paper and then read those papers to me, sharing what she learned in her freshman government classes. I would not have experienced those things but for the global pandemic.

As 2020 progressed, the city of Houston saw more COVID cases, more businesses closing, and more deaths. I received hundreds of calls from people who needed help because they had experienced loss in so many ways. Their stories fueled my desire to be a resource and connect them with the help they needed. In the midst of helping others, I experienced a deep appreciation for the many gifts in my life: a roof over my head, time to walk in nature or just sit still. These are things I didn't necessarily make time for during the hustle and bustle of my sixty- to eighty-hour work weeks.

The extreme and sudden shock of the global shut-down further ignited my passion for people and making a difference in this world in the greatest way possible. I made the choice to appreciate the tools I had, the resources I had, the people in my life, and the gift of time. Having to communicate virtually with colleagues, staff, sponsors, media, and others, felt like a 24/7 endeavor, but I embraced it one hundred percent.

As the world slowly emerged from the pandemic, I could see the fruits of the seeds of passion I had deposited, and I gained a deep appreciation for things that had previously been normal, like going to a restaurant and engaging with people outside of "the COVID bubble" of home. Marisa went back to Columbia University in New York City to complete her mechanical engineering degree, and Mia entered Georgetown University in Washington, DC as a second-year student studying government, both saddled with the new normal of wearing a mask to class and sanitizing their hands multiple times each day to prevent exposure to the deadly coronavirus.

I have a passion for serving and for doing things well, with a sense of urgency and with immense joy. Perhaps because of my parents' sacrifices, or because I've heard the click of a gun held to my head, I appreciate the subtleties of life even in the midst of chaos. Every moment is a reminder that life is short and, therefore, should be lived with passion. My desire is to live a fulfilled life. I owe this to my parents, to myself, and to my daughters.

Persistence

Throughout my career, I have been described as a hard-charger, a go-getter, and someone with endless energy. I learned this from my dad. Watching him run two businesses when I was a kid and seeing how he dealt with people and made decisions influenced me in ways I didn't recognize until I took the time to evaluate my own methods of persuasion and getting to the many yeses I have sought.

Being persistent means finding new ways to articulate a point, to present an idea, and to provide value to the person I'm trying to engage. I have demonstrated persistence time and again in my career, and it has always paid dividends far beyond my expectations.

My favorite song is "Don't Stop Believing," by Journey. I like it so much it has been my onstage walk-up song whenever I speak to large groups. The words of that song are a daily reminder that, no matter what challenges present themselves, I must continue to expect great outcomes. Plans change and circumstances change, but when I remain persistent, great things happen.

———————●———————

The Hispanic Chamber of Commerce hosts an annual luncheon and business expo. During my tenure, and thanks to our board and staff, it became the largest luncheon and business expo in the city with well over 1,600 attendees and an exponential increase in revenue, attendance, and visibility from previous years. One of the highlights of the event is the keynote speaker, typically someone well respected in academia, business, or politics. The Chamber has welcomed such notables as astronaut Scott Kelly, multi-millionaire entrepreneur Jim McIngvale, and the presidents of the top three universities in Texas: Dr. Renu Khator, Chancellor and President of the University of Houston System, Jim Sharp, President of Texas A&M University, and Dr. Francisco Cigarroa, Chancellor of UT System.

LEAD IN LIFE MOMENT

Leverage relationships where you have already proven yourself.

In 2015, I decided to ask Tilman Fertitta, Houston billionaire businessman and owner of the National Basketball Association's Houston Rockets, to be the keynote speaker. First, I asked some of his inner circle whether they thought he would accept the invitation. Their response was: he doesn't do that. It was time to access my network to move this passion project forward. Immediately, I thought of one of my mentors, Dr. Renu Khator, who had been a keynote speaker at the luncheon in the past.

Dr. Khator had invited me to sit on her advisory board. Tilman was the Chairman of the Board of Regents for the University of Houston at the time, so we crossed paths there and at a variety of functions throughout Houston. This was the perfect storm for me to interact with Tilman and others in Houston's philanthropic community.

At one meeting with Dr. Khator, I asked if she would talk to Tilman about the Chamber and encourage him to accept my invitation to serve as our keynote speaker. "Look, I know Tilman doesn't know me," I said, "But I know that if you vouch for me and the Chamber, he might consider accepting the invitation."

"Oh, yes, he does, Dr. Laura," said Dr. Khator. "Tilman knows who you are."

Dr. Khator later invited me to the University of Houston to attend a private lunch with her and the Dean of the UH library. I had no idea why I was asked to join them for what seemed a very formal lunch meeting. To my surprise, Dr. Khator asked that I consider donating my writings, videos, and other works to be archived at the University of Houston, the place where I had earned three degrees and had spent the very early part of my professional career. I was honored by the invitation to donate my body of work to my alma mater, and I humbly agreed. My hope is that these archives will stand as a legacy of my accomplishments and a point of inspiration for my daughters and for others.

Thankfully, my relationship with UH has continued for many years. The University of Houston bestowed its highest honor, the President's Medallion, upon the Chamber and me, making us the first Hispanic organization to receive this honor in UH history. Additionally, I was honored with the 2018 Distinguished Alumni Award. That same year, I was voted the Most Admired CEO by the *Houston Business Journal* and was named Mother of the Year by the Houston Latin Philharmonic, who dedicated an entire performance in my honor, which was coincidentally held in the opulent UH Cullen Pavilion.

For the next three years, I made every effort in my power to secure Tilman Fertitta as our keynote speaker, including sending formal letters requesting that he speak, contacting people who worked with him, and broaching the subject each time I saw him. As a member of the M.D. Anderson Cancer Center board of directors, I was invited to a Christmas fundraiser at Paige and Tilman Fertitta's

> **LEAD IN LIFE MOMENT**
>
> You can't stop after three noes. You have to analyze, assess, and find a new way to present your point. Then, move forward with persistence.

home. I introduced myself to Paige and mentioned the annual luncheon and my request for Tilman to speak. Her response was, "He doesn't do that, but I'm so glad you're here and thanks for all you do for Houston." My tenacity wouldn't allow me to quit. I am a firm believer that sometimes no just means not now. Tilman wasn't a "No." He was a "Not now."

My pursuit of Tilman gained more solid footing when, one day, as I drove past the headquarters of Tilman's company on my way from a meeting, something told me to stop. I stopped at a nearby store and bought a small cake and had "Thank You" written on it in lovely lettering. I took the cake to Tilman's office and was greeted by the security guard.

"Hi, I'm here to see Tilman's assistant," I said in my cheeriest voice.

"Who can I tell her is here?" asked the guard.

"Oh, I'm Dr. Laura Murillo." I had never met her, but I wanted to thank Tilman's assistant for responding to all my emails, letters, and calls.

Before I knew it, she was in the lobby and was all smiles. "Oh, how nice. We finally meet, Dr. Laura," she said. We shook hands, and she continued, "Tilman isn't here."

I smiled, and looked her right in her eyes. "I'm so pleased to meet you," I said. "This isn't for Tilman; this is for you. I just wanted to say thank you. Enjoy the cake." Then, I turned and walked out.

A few weeks later, as the date for the luncheon approached, I received a call from Tilman's executive assistant indicating that he was seriously considering accepting my request. Just two weeks before the luncheon, I was thrilled that my three-year pursuit of Tilman had finally resulted in a yes—well, almost.

All the planning for our 2018 Houston Hispanic Chamber of Commerce Annual Luncheon moved forward without any mention of who the keynote speaker would be, as was customary during my tenure. Two days before the luncheon, Tilman was still only tentative.

Finally, the day of the luncheon arrived. Our staff vice president, Jorge Mancilla, was one of only a few people who knew of our keynote speaker's identity. I asked him to position himself outside the Hilton Americas Hotel and to text me as soon as Tilman arrived. When I received the text, it was show time! Wearing a suit and tie, not his usual more laid-back attire, Tilman entered the ballroom and said to me, "Dr. Laura, everything I heard about you is true. I read your bio. I'm so impressed."

He glanced at all the CEOs seated in the audience, many of whom he recognized because they were people he did business with, influencers in the local business community who were responsible for how the city ran. "Walk with me," he said. "I want to be out there. I want to see who's here. There are so many people I know!" We walked a few paces from the backstage area onto the ballroom floor. Indeed, the Hispanic Chamber was playing with the big boys. We had arrived as a community and earned our place as a full-fledged participant in Houston's economic platform.

"Tilman, I want to thank you and your team," I said. "As a follow-up to this, I want to get together to discuss mutually beneficial opportunities." I was setting the stage for the next phase of our engagement, preparing the Chamber to provide more opportunities for minorities businesses.

I quickly escorted Tilman backstage before stepping onstage to introduce him and his introduction video. The lights dimmed, I exited the stage, and the audience saw the image of Tilman Fertitta getting off his jet. In that moment, he was standing with me in the wings, looking in awe at the audience, their eyes focused on a huge widescreen showing his larger-than-life sizzle reel.

I said to him, "Look at the diversity in this room."

He said, "I do business with so many people here."

As the video ended, Tilman walked out onstage with high energy and confidence. "Look at this organization," he said. "Look at this woman. She's got a bachelor's, a master's, and a doctorate, she's a University of Houston graduate, and she's transformed this organization. She stalked me for three years. She's a persistent one!" The crowd applauded wildly. "You want to be where the excitement is, where the energy is? Well, this is where I want to be because this is where it's at." I'm sure I had the biggest smile on my face by then. But what he said next surprised me. "I was going to become a member of the Italian Chamber of Commerce, but I'm gonna stick to the Hispanic Chamber."

To see Tilman Fertitta's keynote presentation, visit my resources at DrLauraMurillo.com/media

That luncheon was by far one of our most successful. Getting Tilman Fertitta as our keynote speaker taught me so much about myself and about diversity and inclusion. When an organization or leader has preconceived perceptions of a person, a group, or an organization—even if they are unconscious perceptions—

LEAD IN LIFE MOMENT

The biggest part of achieving a goal is the execution. Don't get stuck or turn away after a few noes. Be persistent and push through moments of slow progress. Your reward is on the other side of difficulty.

making meaningful connections can be difficult. After all, taking people seriously and offering a sincere listening ear can seem like it's not worth your time. Not until you step into their space do you appreciate what they bring to the table. But if you never make an effort to meet them where they are, you may never know what value they provide, and as a result, you might miss out on new opportunities for your own organization. Diversity and inclusion are a two-way street. When only one side makes an effort, both sides lose. When both parties come to the table open and respectful of each other, magic can happen.

I continued to cross paths with Tilman at social and business functions, and I followed up with him several times to ask if there was anything the Chamber could do to support him and his executive team. My initial goal was to be a resource for Tilman's empire, not just to have him speak at a luncheon. Following the luncheon, my relationship with his executive team grew even more valuable as we developed a variety of partnership opportunities. I proposed the idea to one of his executives to consider hosting the Chamber, along with sixty CEOs, at a breakfast so I could present information on diversity, equity, and inclusion at Tilman's hotel, the Post Oak, located in the affluent Galleria area of Houston. This was a stellar opportunity for them to showcase their hotel and a chance for me to share a critical message about the importance of DEI for companies and organizations seeking to remain relevant in the twenty-first century.

With the release of Tilman's book, *Shut Up and Listen*, I wanted to share his business lessons with others. Ideally, I wanted him to agree to an interview, which would air on CBS television, with me in his office. He agreed.

During the interview, I asked him, "So, why did you finally agree to speak at the Chamber event?"

"Dr. Laura," he said, "it was your persistence. You're a lot like me." We both laughed. "If you can get me to speak at your event *and* do a local interview, there's just about nothing you can't do."

To see my interview with Tilman Fertitta, visit my resources at DrLauraMurillo.com/media

2020. My interview with Tilman Fertitta in his opulent office aired on CBS KHOU 11.

Tilman Fertitta, billionaire businessman and TV personality, Chairman and CEO of Landry's, and owner of the NBA's Houston Rockets as the 2018 keynote speaker at the Chamber's luncheon.

*My pal and former Houston Chief of Police, Art Acevedo,
with Tilman and me at an Astros game.*

*Tilman shared a nice compliment when autographing
his book,* Shut Up and Listen! *as a gift to me.*

CHAPTER 3

BE BOLD,
BE STRONG

Youngest Director in University of Houston History.

In 1989, I was at the start of my career as a professional, having earned a bachelor's degree in journalism from the University of Houston. My first professional position was serving as Assistant Director for University Outreach for the University of Houston, Texas A&M, and the University of Texas. My role was to recruit and retain minority students to any of the three institutions to increase diversity among their student body.

After just two years in that position, I was recruited to work exclusively for UH. My supervisor was Dr. Tatcho Mindiola, a tenured professor and the Director for The Center for Mexican American Studies (CMAS). Dr. Mindiola had influenced the lives of so many Mexican Americans and Hispanics in Houston. A graduate of Brown University and professor of sociology, he was passionate about his work in race relations and shared his insights in numerous media interviews. Under his tutelage, I learned the importance of understanding the nuances of our culture and the significance of higher education in furthering opportunities for Hispanics and minorities in every sector of business, politics, and economic progress.

In my new role, I had the opportunity to not only do what was in the job description, but to also extend myself beyond that. Having a boss and mentor who understood my desire to do more and to be someone who didn't just show up and do business as usual was critical to my success. Because I was so young, in my mid-twenties, and I interacted with students at the university, I didn't want to be mistaken as a student in my new role. I had to show I was, in fact, a staff person, someone my colleagues saw as an equal who added value to the team. In addition, I wanted other departments and the professors to take me seriously, so I dressed the part and wore suits every day. Some of my mentors—older, more mature women—wore brooches, and I adopted that fashion trend to add to my brand credibility and reputation.

My last official workday at the University of Houston. My mom and daughters joined me at my going away celebration on campus. Go Coogs!

Each year under the direction of Dr. Mindiola, my work improved. I received a promotion every other year, and by age twenty-two, I became the youngest director in UH history. Always focusing on what the job could be and not what it was, was the key to career advancement. I wanted to play a significant role in shaping the direction of the Center and making it a vital part of the university. Every action I took led to a new position with more responsibility. This assertive approach to my work led to being invited to important committee meetings that raised the visibility of the Center and enhanced my own credibility. Making myself available to attend an early-morning or late-night meeting on campus or in the community was a daily occurrence. This allowed me to meet and learn from decision-makers. Meeting with many of the university's directors and with representatives from various sectors in the Houston business community allowed me to provide solutions to meet the needs of the community through the university's many resources. I also hosted and produced an access cable television show which featured CMAS programs and services.

Soon enough, I began to make a name for myself and became involved in more university-wide activities. In short order, I became viewed as someone who took initiative and got things done. That was enough to earn the attention of Dr. James Pickering, President of the University of Houston. One day, he invited me to a meeting.

"Laura, I've been watching your work, and I like your results," he said.

I was flattered and felt as if the extra effort I was putting forward was being recognized.

"Your experience has made the work you're doing successful. Diversity is important to me," Dr. Pickering said. "I would like you to serve as the founding director for a recruitment and retention program called the Urban Experience, sponsored by the office of the president. Would you be interested in heading up a team to develop a student recruitment and retention program for minorities, not just for Hispanics?"

My curiosity was piqued. This sounded like something right up my alley, but my allegiance was with Dr. Mindiola and the Center for Mexican American Studies.

Dr. Pickering explained, "This would be co-sponsored by my office and the Center for Mexican American Studies, with a multi-year financial investment to make sure our freshman class is more diverse."

I was happy to know my office would remain at CMAS. My new salary would be split evenly between CMAS and the office of the president. With the support of other departments, through focus groups and dynamic conversations, the Urban Experience Program was born at the University of Houston. The multi-year funding was great, but it wasn't enough. Building external allies would prove beneficial as I began my position as founding director of the Urban Experience program.

I took it upon myself to organize the center's first fundraising event. We called it Noche Cultural. Negotiating the in-kind use of the university's hotel and alumni facilities would reduce our cost and would not only bring 250 alumni back to campus, but would also bring sponsors. It was a win/win proposition. I utilized every opportunity to brand and market the Urban Experience Program and CMAS. I continued to cultivate and steward relationships outside of the university and seek investments in support of the Urban Experience program.

Due to the extensive work of the Urban Experience Program in its first year, and thanks to the entire CMAS team, enrollment of Hispanic students at the university jumped from thirty-five percent to nearly eighty-five percent for the initial cohort. Many of the students went on to earn a master's degree and at least five earned a doctorate. One of the happiest moments of my life was an invitation to speak at the fundraising gala for the Urban Experience Program. In attendance were members of the initial cohort, about twenty young people we had helped during their junior high, high school, and college experience. They came together for this special occasion and asked me to serve as the keynote speaker. They each took the stage and shared beautiful sentiments about how their lives had been impacted during their time in the program. I was so proud of what they had accomplished. It filled me with gratitude, knowing that I had used my influence and my passion to help others. Their success is a testament to me that I made a difference and left a legacy of caring for people, working with passion, and demonstrating persistence in any endeavor.

By the time I earned my master's degree, I had accepted the promotion as the founding Director of the Urban Experience Program. As the program's founder, my heart and soul were involved in the program, and I saw bright prospects for it. I knew the hard work of the staff would help the program remain vibrant and strong well into the future. Over the years, the program has continued to expand and gain respect on campus and recognition in the city of Houston and throughout academia.

> **LEAD IN LIFE MOMENT**
>
> You are not alone. There are people who want to help you. Find the courage to seek help. Accept their help. Don't be intimidated by their power and knowledge. Ask questions to figure out how things work, and be persistent to achieve what you set out to accomplish.

The program was a first for the university, and there were so many challenges. We recruited students from several middle and high schools in the city, including where I went to school, Edison Junior High and Austin High School. I visited the homes of dozens of high school students who had the potential to attend the university but faced challenges in their personal circumstances that might have threatened their higher-education goals. Some of the girls had parents who expressed concerns about them living on campus. Other students needed support with remedial courses to improve their grade point average. Many of them were the first in their family to graduate high school and attend college. All the students had promise, and I connected with each of them. Additionally, we provided much-needed support for minority students already in the UH system, providing help with course selection, studies, and managing college life and helping them navigate the system.

After seven years of successfully recruiting and retaining minority students, Dr. Pickering acknowledged the progress I had made with the program and encouraged me to seek opportunities outside the department which would expand my reach and impact. Although I appreciated his encouragement, I wasn't ready to change direction in my career. I was comfortable where I was and felt I was at the top of my game. That department was my home base, yet I knew other opportunities awaited me outside of the ethnic experience. Little did I know then my career would soon pivot, and I would enter an entirely new realm within the academic arena.

Being bold and being strong gave me the courage to step out of my comfort zone. Over time, I realized I could be more impactful sitting at the table with people who were not like me to help them understand the needs of minority students. Having critical conversations among a tight-knit group of minority students and staff was a good first step, but others who could take action to improve conditions and fund programs needed to hear from a strong advocate. That advocate was me.

Take Care of the Job You Have and the Next One Will Find You

My reputation was growing and my personal brand becoming more defined as I consistently demonstrated that I was an out-of-the box thinker who could bring people together. In just eight years, my career was on a fast-track trajectory that I could never have planned for myself. Soon, I found myself at a different table with different people, where I learned a new way to support the Center's efforts to enhance its footprint at the university and its impact on minority students. I was recruited for a new position as the Development Director for UH's Advancement and External Relations department. The hardest decision I had to make was leaving the Center for Mexican American Studies because that environment was familiar to me.

Serving others and helping them achieve their goals provided immediate gratification for me, and the interaction I had with the students was energizing. The people who made up those communities were known entities to me, and that provided a sense of comfort. However, to serve them better, and to ensure my own best future, I had to find ways to elevate my role, my knowledge, and my expertise. My next career move, from the Center into a more mainstream role in the President's office through University Advancement and External Relations, allowed me a view of the bigger picture of the university's outreach to minority communities beyond the hands-on details. In a sense, I felt I was abandoning my base, but in actuality, I was elevating my voice to better serve them.

Once I understood the impact I could make in my new role, I was over the fear of being in a new environment and became more comfortable in my seat at the table. The Urban Experience Program would continue without me under the promise that my assistant would step up to the plate and run the program, which would later be renamed the Academic Achiever's Program. True success is empowering others and setting the foundation for something that lasts long after you are gone.

The new role placed me in the center of fundraising opportunities, which impacted programs and services throughout the university. When I was recruited to the University Advancement and External Relations team, I was the only Hispanic development director and, again was blessed with a boss, Spencer Yantis, Vice President of University Advancement and External Relations, who believed in me and provided much-needed training. At this level, I was in a much more influential and powerful position than before because I was able to advocate for more resources to be directed to the Center for Mexican American Studies. Additionally, with the insight I gained from being at the table where funding and allocation decisions were made, I could help the Center understand how the process worked.

LEAD IN LIFE MOMENT

Continuing to build and grow can be difficult and sometimes requires you to remove yourself from a comfortable situation to take on something with more risk. Be bold. Do it anyway. Take the risk. Believe in yourself and your dream.

From that post, I was promoted to Development Director at the College of Education, where I developed creative funding strategies for the college. During my time there, I focused on presidential endowed scholarships. Soon, I was promoted to the College of Business. In the academic world, this was known as the mecca of fundraising for a university's portfolio because entrepreneurs and others who are successful are often donors or have foundations interested in supporting a school of business. The College of Business is also where many corporations are heavily involved as a way to add their fingerprint to the curriculum and scout for top talent.

Learning about fundraising, foundations, and external relations, and how those areas impacted various departments at the university allowed me to serve as a role model for students and other minority professionals at the university because I was one of very few minorities at a table of decision-makers.

A critical part of my personal branding during my fifteen years at the University of Houston was my professional persona. The intention was to conduct myself in a professional way and always do what I said I would do. I established a reputation for myself as someone who got things done. Part of that, I believed, was earning a doctorate. In the various meetings I attended with funders, and with the mentors in my circle of influence, I noticed the decision-makers all had two initials in front of their name. They were the leaders, and I wanted to have the same influence they had as part of my brand.

Invest in Yourself

The life I envisioned for myself was one where I had choices. I saw how hard my parents worked, and I realized education was the foundation for increasing the number of choices available in life. I hoped that serving as a change agent and influencer would have a lasting impact on people. Continuing my education would increase my chances of accomplishing all of this. Pursuing a doctorate degree was the next logical step.

Going back to school when I had a toddler, was working full time, and was advancing in my career faster than I ever expected, seemed to me like a ridiculous idea, yet something inside me let me know I could do it. Before making the final decision to go for it, I consulted with a professor, as a sounding board, to ensure I had as much information as possible to make my decision. His raised eyebrows and the puzzled look on his face prepared me for the barrage of unsupportive questions he fired at me. "Are you quitting your job? What about your family? How will you find the time to study? Does your boss know you're considering this? Do you realize how much it costs to get a doctorate? You do realize most people, like you, who start never finish, right?"

That conversation, completely opposite of the supportive consultation I had hoped for, became the motivation I needed to move forward. Figuring out how to navigate all the aspects of life while earning a doctorate was a challenge I was ready to take on, and yet self-doubt loomed over my head. Even after completing the application, I carried it around in my bag for six months, afraid of not being accepted and concerned that if I was, I wouldn't be able to finish. The curriculum was intimidating, with several statistical analysis courses and others for which I didn't feel prepared.

Finally, I submitted the application, along with my stellar letters of recommendation, and then took my exams and hoped for the best. Unfortunately, my scores were too low to be accepted. I was devastated, but not dissuaded. I persisted and took the exam again. My scores still were not high enough. Always the advocate for myself and others, I meticulously read through the requirements and learned that conditional admission was available for students who would be required to maintain an A average in the first year of the program. Therefore, I appealed their decision and included additional letters of recommendation from community leaders, who vouched for my volunteerism from the age of fifteen, and from colleagues, who highlighted my accomplishments at work. With that, I was admitted into the doctoral program.

LEAD IN LIFE MOMENT

Viewing the totality of your responsibilities can be overwhelming. You don't have to do everything at once. Take one step at a time with each activity, and ultimately, you will reach your goal.

Determined to keep all the balls of my life in the air, and believing what I had dreamed was possible, I was energized to get through the courses and my workday without much sleep. I developed a routine of waking up at three in the morning to do homework for a few hours before preparing breakfast, packing my lunch bag and Marisa's diaper bag, and then grabbing my backpack and heading out the door to drop off the baby and get to the office by eight o'clock. As if all of that wasn't enough to keep me busier than most on a daily basis, I was introduced to a prime opportunity that I couldn't pass up.

Always looking for ways to expand my knowledge of diversity, I decided to apply for a one-month doctoral fellowship at the University of Beijing in China via the UH Asian American Studies Program. Upon acceptance, I became the only Hispanic admitted into the program at that time, an honor that allowed me the opportunity to learn about another rich culture. My professors went out of their way to help me understand and appreciate the customs, culture, and protocol of a country so unfamiliar to me and distinct from my own. Through the engagements I had in various sectors of Chinese society, I gained a deeper understanding of the diversity of that culture and an appreciation for the wealth of diversity throughout world. That experience provided me with a global perspective on life, which would serve me well years later when I joined Mayor Annise Parker as part of a business delegation to China. Having a curiosity about other cultures, and a sincere desire to learn their practices and protocols, has informed my approach to the work I do in diversity, equity, and inclusion.

Back then, not everyone shared my enthusiasm about the trip to China. My mother, for one, felt that, once again, I was doing too much. "What if something happens?" she asked.

My response was: "What could happen?"

No one could have known the flood of a lifetime would occur in Houston while I was gone, leaving the entire city under water and dozens of communities in ruins. As I boarded the airplane on my return to Houston, I opened the front page of a Beijing newspaper and saw the headline "Houston Under Water Due to a Tropical Storm." Each of my fellow students panicked. We all had family in Houston we were looking forward to returning home to, and this news sent us into a whirlwind of emotions. Unable to call home due to downed phone lines and unstable networks, we managed the thirteen-hour flight back to the U.S. while not knowing the status of our families. The tropical storm devastated the city, causing loss of life, loss of businesses, and overwhelming destruction to the infrastructure. Fortunately, my three-year-old daughter and our family were safe, an incredible relief for me. Once the storm clouds cleared and my life returned to my version of normal, I resumed the hectic schedule I had become accustomed to.

Just as a solid routine with work, school, and home life was developing, I received devastating news. My mom had suffered a massive heart attack and was hospitalized. The diagnosis was poor, and she was given three days to live. The doctor said my mom had ninety-five percent blockage in her left artery and our family should prepare for her funeral. I was in shock.

My professor suggested I take medical leave. "Look, you have too much going on," he said. "You're working full time, you're a full-time doctoral student, you have a toddler, you're pregnant with a second child, your mother is gravely ill, and you have to not only pass your comprehensive exams, but you also need to complete your doctoral dissertation. Take care of your family and yourself and come back in a year."

I immediately rejected that as an option. By that time in my life, I already knew one of my strongest characteristics is that when times get tough, I double down on my efforts. With so much on my mind, I didn't even have the words to rebut the professor's advice. I simply left his office and went straight to the intensive care unit at St. Luke's Hospital.

Unable to visit with my mom right away, I sat in the waiting room, took out my giant three-ring binders, and studied for the comprehensive statistical analysis exam. I couldn't heal my mom, but I could focus on my studies. Not surprisingly, I found it difficult to concentrate, so I prayed. I thought about how my parents had crossed the Rio Grande as immigrants all those years ago and how they would want me to keep moving forward. There was no way I could disappoint them by not continuing what I had started. With all sorts of excuses to stop, I made the choice to keep going. Committed to completing my studies, I sat in the intensive care waiting room and studied thousands of pages filled with statistical analysis notes. Their legacy and the future of my growing family were dependent on me earning my doctorate degree.

LEAD IN LIFE MOMENT

Nothing in life is given. You have to work hard to achieve your goals. There is no easy way to do it. Make education a priority and dedicate yourself to serving others. That combination is an almost guaranteed recipe for success.

For weeks, I continued with my studies, focused intently on passing the statistical analysis exam. To say I struggled with every detail of the coursework would be an understatement. All my efforts to absorb the material didn't seem to amount to a greater understanding. I recorded the lectures and replayed them during my daily commute to work. I transferred my notes to Post-its and placed them throughout my home. I scribbled formulas on slips of paper and affixed them to my walls, on the microwave, everywhere. I listened to class audiotapes to and from work and during every meal. I hired tutors and participated in study-group meetings. When my peers left, I remained until the library closed late in the evening. I was always the first to arrive and the last to leave. Doing all this was the choice I made in order to finish what I had started.

With my mother still in the hospital, I took the exam and waited for the results. Pregnant for the second time and working full time, I was relieved this one hurdle had been crossed so I could focus on the other important things in my life. Waiting for the test results was excruciating.

Within days, the dean called me to share the results. Only four of the forty students who took the test had passed, he informed me. "You're one of the four, Laura. Congratulations."

I wanted to believe him, I really did, but with so much going on in my life, I was hesitant to celebrate. I responded, "Please check my social security number again to make sure I actually passed."

"Don't worry," he said. "We double checked. You passed, you passed, you passed!"

The sacrifices I made to pass that test were extreme, but they were part of my natural approach to a challenge. Going above and beyond, controlling what I could control, compartmentalizing tasks, and persisting at something until it's done, are all elements of doing things my way. Passing that five-hour written exam and successfully defending my doctoral dissertation were the final steps to earning my doctorate.

My mother lived through the heart attack to see me, her youngest daughter, cross the stage and earn a doctorate, just months after giving birth to Mia, my second born. My mom was so proud to see I had created a life filled with choices she didn't have, choices that opened new doors of opportunity for myself and for my daughters. The opportunities were for us to share, but I always wanted my girls to know earning my doctorate was my sacrifice, not theirs.

From the time they were born, Marisa and Mia were my sources of inspiration for accomplishing my goals. As they grew up, I wanted them to adopt the belief that they could do anything they set their mind to, so each morning, we would declare our mantra: "You are smart, you are beautiful, and God loves you." By their teen years, they tired of the practice, but I made sure we did it anyway because it mattered to me, and I knew someday it would matter to them.

No matter how many eighteen-hour days I worked, I made sure to be there for them whenever they needed me. The pace of their activities picked up in tandem with mine, with school programs and trips, homework, and special projects. Over the years, I have been so proud to watch them accomplish their own goals, and I wanted to make sure they knew that, despite the hectic pace of my life, I was watching and was well pleased. I did this by writing notes to each of them from the time they were born and placing those notes in a box I tucked away. For each goal they realized, each project they completed, each acknowledgement they received, I wrote a note expressing how proud I was. When each of them turned eighteen, I gave them their box of love notes. They had no idea I had been doing this over the years. Those notes were a testament to them that my biggest job was being their mom. The girls and my mom saw, firsthand, how my educational pursuits led to more choices, not only for me, but for them as well.

Reach Your Full Potential

Prior to completing my doctorate in Administration and Supervision from the University of Houston's College of Education, where I had earned a master's and a bachelor's degree, several executive search firms began contacting me with job opportunities. My career goal was to stay at the University of Houston and continue to move up, eventually to the role of vice president. God had other plans for me, even though I didn't realize it at the time.

One of the organizations that reached out was Memorial Hermann Hospital and Children's Memorial Hermann Hospital in Texas Medical System, the largest not-for-profit health system in southeast Texas. The executive recruiters suggested to Juanita Romans, the CEO of Memorial Hermann, that she should interview me. I had already done my research on Memorial Hermann and Juanita, so I had good insight into the requirements and expectations of the position. The interview was professional yet personable, and Juanita and I communicated with an ease that was refreshing. Within the first five minutes, I knew I wanted to work with her. She wasted no time explaining why she thought I would be a good fit for the position, and I listened intently without interrupting.

When she finished, I asked one simple question. "Why should I leave the University of Houston, to come to work for you?"

Her reply was simple and sincere. "Because I develop people, and I want to develop you."

My daughters, Marisa and Mia, at my UH doctoral graduation. Full-time mom, full-time UH employee, and full-time UH doctoral student.

That resonated with me because there had been so many people who had already developed me as a professional and embraced my creativity, helping me arrive where I was at that point in my career. Their influence had ignited in me the desire to help others advance in their careers. In a sense, it was akin to a "pay it forward" approach to talent development, and there I was, right in the middle of the game. Knowing Juanita's desire was to help me reach my fullest potential as a professional mattered so much to me. If there was a time for me to move to the next opportunity, this was the time, this was the place, and this was the woman I believed could help me get there.

The idea of moving into an entirely different business sector and a more high-profile position was intimidating, but I was willing to consider the opportunity. Again, I had choices. I could remain at the University of Houston, or I could move on. The choice was difficult for me. The opportunities and experiences I enjoyed at the university had nurtured my skills and helped me grow into a leader and a role model. I was proud of the meaningful impact I'd had on the students and the minority communities I served. The university was my comfort zone, but I knew from my experience years earlier that remaining in the comfort zone is not a place of growth. I had to spread my wings and reach for more. Despite my fears of leaving my comfort zone and my baby, the Urban Experience Program, I was ready to gain more experience in another space with other people.

I accepted the position as a Senior Director responsible for Fundraising and External Relations for Memorial Hermann Hospital and Children's Memorial Hermann in the Texas Medical Center. I was one of ten people on the executive team reporting to the CEO. That was one of the best decisions I have made in my career.

Months passed, and I learned the ropes at Memorial Hermann, how decisions were made, when and whether to speak up and when to sit back and listen. As one of the youngest members of the executive committee, and the only Hispanic, I wanted to establish myself as a valuable resource the team could rely on to get results. Sometimes that meant volunteering for projects on top of an already full plate of responsibilities. On more than one occasion, I raised my hand to step into what was considered the grunge work. On every occasion, I did my best to demonstrate to the team that I was a team player and I was willing to learn and to serve.

Over time, my voice became that of the patient experience. For example, signage is a critical aspect of navigating the campus for patients and families, given the size of the hospital. When others in the department discussed the clinical aspects of service delivery, I asked what those areas would mean to patients. In many meetings, I remained silent, merely listening and learning. When I did speak up, my colleagues would say, "Oh, we didn't think of it that way." Their perspective was usually that of a clinician; mine was that of a patient or family member. Among the many lessons I learned while working there was that hospitals are a 24/7 operation (pun intended). Maintaining a high level of patient care was an ongoing effort, and I was honored to share my perspectives to improve outcomes for every patient and family that came through our doors.

When Juanita brought up the United Way campaign at an executive team meeting, I could see by the body language of everyone at the table that no one wanted to head up the project. Everyone else on the team had led the campaign in years past and understood the time commitment to successfully execute it. Ever eager to step up to the plate, I jumped at the opportunity. Heading up this project meant reaching out to employees in every department to encourage their donations to the organization's annual giving campaign. I understood exactly what that equated to in terms of more work for me, but I saw an opportunity to stand out and demonstrate that I was a team player and to relieve my colleagues of the responsibility of this important community project. The role would also provide me with the opportunity to meet leaders of different departments at the hospital and to reconnect with a similar type of work I had done with the Center for Mexican American Studies at the University of Houston.

As the lone non-clinician on the executive committee at Memorial Hermann, the only Hispanic, and the only one who did not have a degree in hospital administration, I did my best to prove myself. Everyone on the team was well respected in the field, including professionals like Dr. Heather Kopecky, who had been a nurse before she earned a master's degree and a PhD and went on to serve as a partner and executive recruiter at the internationally recognized management consulting firm Korn Ferry. Each Friday was casual day, and most of the team would wear their Memorial Hermann polo shirts and khakis. Always the observer, I noticed the CEO always wore a suit, even on Fridays. So I did the same. My success plan included always looking the part of the job I wanted, not the job I already had. I chose to dress professionally in a suit every day, even on Fridays, because I always wanted to look professional in any situation. Sure enough, an opportunity to support Juanita presented itself on a Friday.

LEAD IN LIFE MOMENT

As you enter the workforce, there will be opportunities for you to take on responsibilities in addition to your day-to-day activities. Evaluate each opportunity to determine if it will lead you closer to your goals. If it can, stand up, speak up, and act with urgency. You never know where it might lead you.

She'd received an urgent call that a CEO had been flown in on a Memorial Hermann Hospital Life Flight helicopter, and she wanted to greet his family and other executives to assure them their VIP would be well cared for. She came into the office and said, "I have to attend a meeting, and I need someone to join me." As she took stock of the team, she noticed everyone was dressed in their typical casual Friday attire—that is, everyone except me. That day, I was clad in a black suit, crisp white blouse, and black pumps. I was ready. "Laura, let's go," she said, motioning for me to follow her.

As we walked across campus, several people we passed greeted me cordially, and Juanita asked how it was that I knew so many people. Through my role managing the United Way campaign, I'd met employees at all levels throughout the hospital system. I was personable and friendly, and they remembered that. One of my keys to opening doors and raising funds was connecting with people in a very authentic way. Juanita was impressed with that.

With my notebook in hand, I accompanied her to the meeting as her handler, where I had the chance to demonstrate to her, and anyone else who might be observing me, that I was all about business. While she was engaging with the executives, I recorded details, writing down names of key contacts, collecting business cards, and noting important information I believed she would need for follow-up. That day, she saw me in action, and I earned my stripes as a professional, someone she could count on.

My role in fundraising and external relations gave me the opportunity to meet an entirely different level of leaders and to understand how their values tied into their level of giving through United Way. As I reported back to Juanita, she was pleased with my approach of engaging with donors who were willing to fund our department's programs. Despite what I might have lacked in terms of my knowledge of hospital administration, the neurosciences, heart research, or the Children's Hospital, I continued to expand my knowledge base and my contacts. As a result, the level of gifts we were able to solicit increased exponentially. My confidence grew as I proved my value with every success I achieved. My role on the team and my ability to perform were never questioned because I demonstrated I could get the job done and because my boss believed in me.

Juanita knew it was important I understand the way the hospital system worked and that I approach my outreach to donors from a fresh perspective. I did just that by drawing upon what I'd learned at the University of Houston through the Urban Experience Program. The practical knowledge I gained at UH about developing services at an institution with a focus on the recipient came in handy.

LEAD IN LIFE MOMENT

Know what kind of people you need on your team to be successful. Think deeply about this before hiring subordinates or entering a mentoring relationship. Be open to people who don't look or think like you. They might offer a needed perspective you might never otherwise consider.

At the University of Houston, my emphasis was helping minority students navigate the educational system. The perspective with which I developed my role in External Relations at Memorial Hermann was through the lens of the patient, who was ultimately the recipient of the services we offered.

My mentor and boss, Juanita Romans, CEO, Memorial Hermann Hospital - Texas
Medical Center (second from right), and our colleagues at Saks Fifth Avenue for my
induction as an ABC-13 Woman of Distinction.

Say You Are and You Shall Become

When I arrived at Memorial Hermann, my career aspiration was to become a vice president, and I believed Juanita Romans could help me get there. As I moved into my career, I saw people who were progressing through their careers swiftly. The next step seemed to have already been laid out for them. I saw myself on the same career trajectory. For them, vice president seemed to be the pinnacle of success, so I aspired to be a vice president at some point in my career. Vice president of what, I didn't know, but I thought that was a high enough goal without having the full responsibility of the next title, which in my mind was president or CEO.

I thought I'd make a solid vice president. Little did I know that Memorial Hermann was in the midst of changing the leadership titles. Eventually, vice president would become system administrator, and when I learned of that change, I was devastated. Nevertheless, I was laser focused on advancing in my career, but at my own pace. So when Juanita called me into her office to discuss a new role, I was cautious. Whether because she saw some untapped potential in me or because of my willingness to take on new responsibilities, she was ready to propel me into the next level of my career.

"Laura, you're not doing fundraising anymore," she stated. Initially, I was confused.

"Yes, I am," I replied assuredly.

She smiled, pleased with my insistence, but certain of her decision. "You're a leader, a people person," she said. "You have a lot of really good skills. It's time you expand and learn other skills."

Her compliment came at a great time in my career. Although my area consisted only of myself and one staffer, the results we achieved were quite notable. Juanita regarded my position and results as critical to the department's success, and she understood the value of what that position could bring. She also knew the time had come for me to spread my wings. My confidence in my ability to connect authentically and professionally with donors and explain the benefits of their involvement in Memorial Hermann was something she appreciated.

"You're going to be a CEO one day," she said. "You need to learn other things, and I want to help you learn those things." The comment came unexpectedly. Knowing she saw CEO potential in me was both flattering and frightening. The rising-star Laura appreciated Juanita's confidence in me, but the laser-focused Laura didn't see beyond VP, so CEO seemed like an impossibility. The pathway to CEO that she charted for me included a move into operations.

LEAD IN LIFE MOMENT

Sometimes your dreams, as big as you might think they are, may not be as big as they can be. Other people with the right intentions have the capacity to see in you what you might not see in yourself. Be open, alert, and ready for the next great opportunity in your career.

Within three years of beginning my role as senior executive director, I transitioned into a brand-new role she created for me, system administrator. That placed me over ten departments, overseeing five hundred employees, with responsibility for a $300 million budget. Within that role, I oversaw everything related to customer relations, international services, VIP patient care suites and waiting rooms, interpreter services, and other patient-facing services. Better still, the new role built my experience managing bigger budgets and performance indices. I was responsible for reviewing profit and loss statements, managing systems and processes, evaluating customer scores, and much more. In many ways, those responsibilities seemed outside my realm of experience because I had never done any of that. In reality, everything I had done in my career was about people, and that was my strong suit.

Aside from my work in Houston, I traveled internationally with Juanita to expand the reach of Texas Medical Center into other countries, including Mexico. We met with elected officials and others to discuss partnerships with other hospitals in an effort to bring more patients to the VIP Signature Suites, for which I was responsible. With each international trip, I gained a greater appreciation for the world-renowned reputation of Texas Medical Center and Memorial Hermann. When I took the job there years earlier, I hadn't imagined I would have these opportunities, but I capitalized on my strengths and every new experience and continued to build a portfolio of leadership credits with each new responsibility.

On a daily basis, it was amazing that I was being entrusted with it all, and I believed I could learn and do an outstanding job, but not because I was experienced at any of this. I wasn't. I believed in myself because Juanita believed in me, and that made all the difference for my success in that position. Her gift for developing the best in people, and specifically for

LEAD IN LIFE MOMENT

Market yourself by serving others and being a source of knowledge. Be the go-to person with information and connections that can benefit others. This is how you get noticed by those who can support and guide you.

developing talent in women, continues to inspire me to this day. To her credit, eight out of ten of the people on her executive committee became CEOs. I was fortunate to work with some exceptional, hard-working professionals on the executive committee who were smart and who cared about the work they did and the people they impacted. Juanita was focused on professional development and invested in herself by hiring an executive coach. Later, she invested in executive coaching for her entire team. As a leader, she allocated financial resources from her department to further develop us individually and collectively. This was her way of demonstrating her commitment to diversity, equity, and inclusion.

People within the Houston business community were taking note of me and my abilities, unbeknownst to me. In my early twenties, I had begun volunteering at the Houston Hispanic Chamber of Commerce and was eventually asked to serve on the board of directors. As one of only three women on the board, I offered ideas and sought solutions for the serious challenges facing the Chamber. When I was asked to head up the annual gala fundraiser, one of the organization's largest events, which was just four months away, I grappled with how I could pull off the event in such a short time, but I agreed to take it on. The thrill of the challenge invigorated me.

While still at Memorial Hermann, and by approaching Juanita Romans and her boss, Dan Wolterman, I secured $25,000 for the Chamber's annual gala. That became an opportunity to showcase Memorial Hermann and its supportive leaders. I used my vacation time to plan the event and still managed to perform the duties of my full time job by working around the clock on both. With the fundraising goal exceeded and all plans in place, the event went off without a hitch.

Meeting with the board of directors afterward, they expressed their sincere pleasure with how well the event was executed. A few board members approached me and suggested that with the skills and focus I had demonstrated with that single event, I could lead the organization into a bright future. As grateful as I was for their vote of confidence, leading an organization like the Chamber was not on my radar. I already had a great career working with a phenomenal boss, so I had no reason to consider leaving. Within a few days of that board meeting, however, my mind took over and I began to see a vision of what was possible for the Chamber if certain things were aligned.

LEAD IN LIFE MOMENT

You can do the bare minimum and get by, or you can do more and get noticed. Utilize your entire palette of skills, talents, and energy to do such an incredible job that when you leave, people will notice. If you leave and no one talks about what you did when you were in that role, and what it will take to replace you, then you might not be working hard enough. Whatever your role, be the best.

The idea of leading the Chamber became a real possibility for me, but I needed to bounce the idea off the great minds within my circle of influence. Individually, I spoke with Dr. Mindiola, Juanita Romans, and a few other trusted mentors to gain their insights about me leading the Chamber. Their advice was split. Some said yes, do it, take the reins. Others said no, there are too many challenges to overcome. In all honesty, those challenges and my vision for how I could help the Chamber overcome them were the deciding factor for me accepting the position as CEO of the Houston Hispanic Chamber of Commerce.

The advice that had the greatest impact on my decision came from Juanita Romans. "You've been preparing for this your whole life, Laura, and you don't even realize it," she said. Her words touched my heart and caused me to reflect on my entire career. She was right. From my work at the University of Houston in the Center for Mexican American Studies department, the creation of the Urban Experience Program, and the results I influenced in External Relations to my experience at Memorial Hermann, I had amassed a treasure of practical knowledge that could be applied at the Chamber. Her belief in me gave me the courage to say yes. Many years later, I asked the board to consider Juanita for a seat on the board. They agreed, and voted her onto the board. She was later elected chairman of the board, becoming the first non-Hispanic to hold that title.

The idea of returning to my passion for serving people and community and facing challenges invigorated me. I could see there were board members poised for a change in leadership and that they were ready to move in a new direction. I believed that running the Chamber as a business, not as a non-profit, would be key to its future success.

In leadership, it's important to see the value of every individual within your organization. Pay close attention to each member of your team, and take note of the go-getters. Give everyone the opportunity to shine. Don't assume that those who lack the industry background, educational credentials, or work experience are not able to step up to the plate. Developing an equitable environment, where each team member is assessed based on their individual skills, knowledge, and experience, has the potential to pay big dividends for your organization. In the new era of inclusion, smart leaders consider and embrace various points of view and understand that those insights can become a competitive advantage.

Building and nurturing trusting, productive relationships works both ways. As you expect employees to reach out to you and others in prominent positions within your organization for advice and guidance, you too should be open to exploring the insights of those rising stars who demonstrate the spirit of innovation and persistence. You will be surprised at the perspectives others on your team have that you might have overlooked because, in the past, everyone has arrived at the table with the same background and point of view. When you give others the opportunity to shine, you and your organization can receive an

> **LEAD IN LIFE MOMENT**
>
> Have accountability partners who have done or are doing what you want to do and who know what it's like to be where you want to be. Gain experience and wisdom from those who are already there. It's fine to share your vision with others, but for the strategy, go to those who have done it.

abundance of new ideas for growth and innovation. Practice listening to those who are not like you and who demonstrate a willingness to go the extra mile.

GALLERY

Family first. Joined my daughters for lunch at Annunciation Orthodox School in the Montrose area of Houston.

My daughters, Mia and Marisa at St. John's School in River Oaks. It is ranked among the top elite private schools in Texas and is ranked #1 in Houston.

My daughters, Marisa and Mia home from Columbia University and Georgetown University.

*By age six, Marisa, taught herself to knit. Years later, she knit this
sweater. Her strong hands sawed all the metal car frame for the
Shell Eco Marathon International Competition. She became the
first Latina president of the St. John's Engineering Club.*

*At age 16, Mia was the youngest congressional intern in Washington,
DC. She worked for Congresswoman Lizzie Fletcher. She also worked as
a Latino constituency organizer. She maintains highest honors at
Georgetown University in Washington, DC.*

After years of trying, I secured an English language radio program on six CBS stations (now Audacy; 3 million plus audience reach). Houston Mayor Annise Parker was among our many guests.

In the CBS Radio (Audacy) studio. Guests include entrepreneurs, educators, CEOs, elected officials, and diverse community leaders.

Diversity Champion. Bobby Springer, CBS KHOU 11, General Manager and VP. We filled the studio with guests for our 10-Year Anniversary Celebration and contract extension. Serving as Founding Executive Producer and Host is an honor.

Speaking alongside Houston's diverse leaders at City Hall.

Advocating for the civic and business interests of Houston at City Hall.

Diversity Champion. Sarah Frazier, Audacy (formerly CBS Radio), Sr. Vice President and Market Manager and I interview mayoral candidates.

During a Cultural Reception at the White House, President Obama requested a private meeting regarding comprehensive immigration. Gloria Estefan and I were among the handful of national leaders escorted by the secret service to meet with him privately.

President Obama visits Houston. I introduce myself by saying, "Houston. Comprehensive Immigration Reform," instead of using my name.

2016. My thanks to Chamber intern, Samanta Rojas, Notre Dame graduate, for the opportunity to serve as keynote speaker for Latino graduates and their families.

Keynote speaker for YES Prep College Signing Day at the Toyota Center, home of the NBA Houston Rockets with 13,000 + attendees.

2018 University of Houston Distinguished Alumni Honoree. Joined by friends, Dr. David and Blanca González, Mayor Sylvester Turner, Dr. Dorothy Caram, and mentor Dr. Renu Khator, UH Chancellor.

2018 Mother of the Year Award from the Latino Philharmonic. Telemundo Anchor, Carlos Robles and Conductor, Glenn Garrito.

Named among the 2018 Most Admired CEOs by the Houston Business Journal. With my pal, Bob Charlet, HBJ Publisher.

Gonzalez Family

One of Magnolia Parks' First Families of restauranteurs, the José González family, would establish itself way before the success of El Jardín Restaurant. José was a very gifted tile mason before his new career. Considered a very distinguished man, José would bring people together with his style, talents and sense of community. Daughter, Dr. Laura Murillo, remembers her father as a man "who saw no barriers, no obstacles."

Houston Community College honored my parents as part of Houston's East End, Magnolia Park legacy families. The college produced a video which is archived and available to the public. I only wish my parents had been alive to accept this honor.

Rest in peace, Big Brother, Joe F. González, Jr.

Mexico's Consul General, Oscar Rodriguez, presents me with The Ohtli Award — the highest honor bestowed by the Mexican government to a Mexican American for their advocacy and civic leadership. Humbled to receive a standing ovation from 1200 attendees.

Exciting day! Enjoyed being part of the NFL Houston Texans coin toss in Reliant Stadium. Full-house of 70,000+ attendees.

My CBS KHOU TV and radio interview with Houston Astros, Jose Altuve, 2017 World Series Champions.

The National Football League (NFL) honors me with the Leadership Award at the NRG Stadium, 70,000 attendees at Houston Texans game.

2020. Diversity Champion, Jamey Rootes, National Football League-Houston Texans, President joins me for an interview on CBS KHOU 11 and on six CBS radio stations with an audience reach 3 million+.

Houston Fire Department Chief Sam Peña and wife Carolina, Sergio and Tiffany Dávila, (Ret) Major General Rick Noriega, Dr. Margo Melcher and John Hernandez.

Neil Bush talks about the Barbara Bush Literacy Foundation on The KUBE. I'm honored to serve as the Founding Executive Producer and Host of Houston Legends.

1989 University of Houston, BA Journalism Degree.

University of Houston, Center for Mexican American Studies students.
Honored to have served as the first staff sponsor of KAX sorority.

Champion. Dr. Tatcho Mindiola, my mentor and former University of Houston boss supports me by attending a Chamber event. He always reminds me that he discovered me.

Due to COVID-19 restrictions, interviews with guests such as Robert Kaplan, President of the Dallas Federal Reserve Board, were recorded via Zoom. The television and radio shows aired on CBS KHOU 11 and CBS Radio (Audacy).

I joined Mayor Annise Parker and business leaders on an international delegation visit to Istanbul, Turkey hosted by the Greater Houston Partnership.

Turkey. Blessed to have traveled the globe representing women.

2020 - Top 30 Texas CEO for exceptional leadership during COVID-19.

Local, state, national media interviews including ABC's Town Hall.

2018. Advocating in support of a Harris County disparity study which would provide data regarding contracts awarded to MWBEs.

Joined Greater Houston Partnership team, Mayor Turner and Port Houston, Chair, Janiece Longoria in Buenos Aires, Argentina to promote international trade.

2021. Historic day at Port Houston, The International Port of Texas. Harris County and Port Houston establish the Business Equity Advisory Council. (Left to Right) Harris County Commissioner Adrian Garcia, Port Houston Commissioner Cheryl Creuzot, Ingrid Robinson HMSDC, Roger Gunther, Port Houston Executive Director, Mayor Sylvester Turner, Port Commissioner Wendy Montoya Cloonan, and Harris County Commissioner Rodney Ellis. Honored to serve on the council and to have advocated for MWBEs alongside these and other leaders.

Appointed to the Port Houston (The International Port of Texas) Business Equity Diversity Council.

Spending ten minutes with billionaire entrepreneur, Warren Buffett, Chairman and CEO of Berkshire Hathaway to discuss the Goldman Sachs 10,000 Small Businesses was surreal.

My interview with NASA Astronaut, Dr. Ellen Ochoa, the first Hispanic woman to go to space.

Champion. Dolores Huerta, Co-Founder of the American Farmers Federation. My thanks to Dr. Kelly Zuniga, President and CEO of the Holocaust Museum, for including us on the panel.

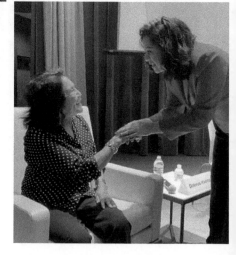

Diversity Champion and my pal, Gerald Smith, Chairman and CEO of Smith Graham Company and Investment Advisors joins me on the Houston Legends TV program.

2021. The Houston Business Journal *honors The Houston Hispanic Chamber of Commerce with two Diversity Awards. Photo includes board members, corporate sponsors, emerging leaders, staff, and volunteers.*

Founding Executive Producer and Host on Spanish language radio and television program on Univision and Unimás.

Film crew interviews me in my office regarding diversity, equity, and inclusion.

ENGLISH LANGUAGE TELEVISION

ENGLISH LANGUAGE RADIO

SPANISH LANGUAGE TELEVISION & RADIO

(3 million cumulative audience reach)

Proud to serve as the Founding Executive Producer and Host on these television and media outlets with a 3 million audience reach.

*Serving as Founding Executive Producer and Host on six
CBS radio stations.*

*University of Houston's Presidential Medallion presented to
the Houston Hispanic Chamber (first Hispanic organization
to receive the honor).*

Mexican President, Vicente Fox, discusses international trade.

University of Houston Golf Tournament with U.S. President George Bush.

Mayor Sylvester Turner hosts Mexican President Felipe Calderon. Harris County Sheriff, Ed González, and I attend the private meeting.

Private meeting with Mexican President, Enrique Peña.

Champions. Edgar Colon, Dr. Stephen Klineberg, George Y. González, and Gilbert Herrera led the Chamber's 2008 Strategic Plan and charged me with leading the execution of the plan. I credit current and former board members and staff for the Chamber's success.

My thanks to our board, staff, sponsors, and volunteers for their support in making the Houston Hispanic Chamber of Commerce Annual Luncheon and Business Expo the largest in Houston with over 1600 attendees.

Diversity Champion, my pal, Paul Murphy, Chairman and CEO of Cadence Bank. In 2017, Paul invited me to the New York Stock Exchange for their initial public offering. Our Chamber elected Paul as the first white male to serve as our board chairman.

2020. Admitted into the Harvard University Women on Corporate Boards Executive Program along with women from across the globe.

My thanks to John Arnold and Chris Canetti for the opportunity to serve on the Board of Directors for the 2026 FIFA World Cup Houston Bid Committee. This brings potentially billions in economic activity and global media exposure for the Greater Houston region.

Bloomberg interviews Mayor Sylvester Turner and me regarding Houston's diversity.

National media coverage.

Superbowl Fox & Friends. Advocating for business on the national media stage.

International Business Delegation in Brazil with Chicago Mayor, Richard Daley and Columbus Mayor, Michael Coleman. The event was co-sponsored by The Brookings Institute and JPMorgan Chase. Chairman and CEO, Jamie Dimon and Vice President, Gina Luna, both of JPMorgan Chase, led the delegation.

Greater Houston Partnership and City of Houston International Trade Mission to Chile, Argentina, and Peru with Diversity Champion, Mayor Sylvester Turner and Houston's business leaders.

Humbled to receive the Global 7 Impact Award from the Houston International Trade Development Council.

Proud graduate of Edison Junior High School, Houston Independent School District.

Proud graduate of Austin High School, Houston Independent School District.

I received Asian American Studies Doctoral Fellowship at the University of Beijing in China.

In China with Mayor Annise Parker-International Trade Delegation. My second trip to China.

Three hundred plus Emerging Leader Institute Graduates. Proud to serve as the Founding President and CEO. Special thanks to all of our current and past board members and staff.

2017 Houston Hispanic Chamber of Commerce Gala (the largest in Houston). Greater Houston Hispanic Chamber of Commerce Foundation Emerging Leader Institute graduates.

Sports Authority Awards Gala board members Chad Burke, Cindy Clifford, Joseph Callie, Kenny Friedman, Janis Burke, Robert Woods, and Larry Catuzzi.

Chad Burke, Robert Woods, Chris Canetti, Janis Burke, Willie Alexander, and Mayor Pro Tem Dave Martin.

*First Latina to serve as an officer on the Harris County-Houston
Sports Authority Executive Committee.*

CHAPTER 4

WORK WITH URGENCY

Because of so many experiences in my life—being held at gunpoint; watching my dad, my hero, die; my mom suffering a massive heart attack—I am committed to living with passion, which creates an urgency in everything I do. Whether I am planning an event, preparing for a meeting, directing staff, or enjoying my family, the way I approach tasks gets me the greatest result in the shortest time. I apply my "work with urgency" approach to everything I do because it works for me. As author Suzanne Evans states, "The way you do anything is the way you do everything." That is certainly true of the way I live life, with urgency.

My life is a constant barrage of activities in various stages of completion. To some, it might appear overwhelming, but it isn't for me because I have developed a straightforward and almost instinctive way of managing the multiple to-dos on my list. Quite simply, I compartmentalize activities. While studying for my doctorate degree, working full time, caring for my ailing mother, and expecting baby number two, I realized I can't do everything at the same time, but I can own how I spend my time. Waking up as early as three in the morning to accomplish as much as I can in the time I have, and not getting distracted by frivolous activities or other people's demands, is my modus operandi. I have learned to be conscious and intentional about life and to try my best to work with urgency.

The Way You Do Anything Is the Way You Do Everything

Multitasking has gotten a bad rap in recent years. Trying to do multiple unrelated activities at the same time can be difficult. Generally, when one thing takes focus, other things might have to be pushed to the side. This is not my experience. My approach to work allows me to work with urgency in everything I do.

Writing things down is imperative when I am working with urgency. I know I cannot do an entire project at once, so making lists and jotting down notes is the way I process my very busy mind. Like the diamond bracelet hidden within the box of rotten tomatoes that my dad gave me, I understand I have to work hard and sometimes sift through the rubbish to reach a goal. Accomplishing anything requires sacrifice and tenacity. There are steps to reach the end game, and I have learned to find joy in completing each task on my list by scratching it out and considering it done and then moving on to the next.

Working with urgency requires eliminating what is no longer important and delegating what others can do. In this way, I apply maximum effort to execution and remain focused. I don't look at an hour as an hour. I look at it as how many things can I do in sixty minutes. That creates a sense of urgency because the hour will pass whether I accomplish twelve things or one. So for me, time is a race to accomplish as much as I can. Working from a list, although not as structured as it might seem, keeps down the confusion and allows me to prioritize activities so I always address the most pressing issues first each day, week, and month. With items prioritized in list form, they can be checked off as I accomplish them and reference them to make sure everything is done. In that way, I take one step at a time toward completion of a goal.

With goals always well-defined and top of mind, I focus on my end game, the results to be achieved, and the outcomes, not only for me, but also for those I serve. What will happen if all these things get done? What is the takeaway? Who will be impacted by the work I'm doing and how? Essentially, I am asking myself, "What is the end game?" Focusing on the end throughout the process of accomplishing anything pushes me forward and makes the victory celebration that much more enjoyable. The end game starts at the beginning of the game when I ask myself, "Do you really want to do this? Is it important? If so, are you willing to endure and overcome the potential bumps in the road?" Answering these questions honestly allows me to move forward with confidence that I will endure and succeed.

The New Era of DEI

Like a set of building blocks, my career has progressed from one new position to the next, one exciting accomplishment to another, each one as critical as the previous and the next in working to make a difference. Individually, these accomplishments are mere actions; each effort stands on its own. As a composite, they represent the aggregate of my passion and my persistence. My reputation has been built one person at a time, one commitment at a time, one action at a time. The commitments I make and the way I execute have become the brand people associate with me. The same is true for corporations with their brand as it relates to diversity, equity, and inclusion.

As my career advanced from one leadership position to the next, I adopted a particular interest in and perspective on diversity practices in corporate settings. Having been the first or the only Hispanic, many times the youngest, and sometimes one of only a few women at the table in many corporate settings, my perspective of diversity, equity, and inclusion has been greatly influenced by my lived experiences. As a leader, I understand we all bring our whole selves into a corporate setting or an organizational situation. I cannot separate the fact that I am Latina, a woman, a mom, and a daughter of immigrants from the fact that I am a president, a CEO, a founder, a board member, and a media personality. In every interaction, I bring the totality of who I am to the table, and I expect others to do the same, all while respecting each other's backgrounds, experiences, abilities, and contributions. That is what the new era of diversity, equity, and inclusion demands.

In this new era of DEI, the concept of diversity means making a solid, long-term commitment to full representation of all voices in every decision at every level of an organization, all the time. Equity means everyone at the table has a fair shot at the same opportunities. Different from equality, which establishes similar resources for various groups, equity actually requires an organization to acknowledge that there are those who have been previously underserved and unrepresented, and then to intentionally eliminate any barriers to participation so everyone has a fair opportunity, in addition to having equal access to equal resources. Inclusion means ensuring everyone who has been invited to the table feels welcome in the environment and all participants accept that every voice must be heard in order for progress to be made.

Today's innovative companies understand the benefits of having a sound and intentional DEI strategy that includes men, women, minorities, and others who have not traditionally been invited to participate in decision-making circles. Traditionally, the people around the table—whether in board meetings, at the executive level, or in funding situations—have been those who are familiar to each other, either through other board positions, in social settings, or by recommendation from a mutual colleague. This long-held practice has illuminated an alarming and obvious lack of diversity, equity, and inclusion in practically every facet of business and society. The issue for many companies and organizations is not a disinterest in implementing DEI practices, but rather a lack of real insight into how to do it. In short, they know they need diversity, they understand why equity is important, and they seek to be inclusive, but they have no intentional long-term approach to make any of that happen.

Considering that white men have most often been the leaders of the corporate "old boys network" it's no wonder corporate boards and executive teams have reflected that demographic. Twenty-first century companies with an inclusive and future-focused approach to growth understand their employees and their consumer base. They realize the urgency and necessity of being in alignment with not only the demographics of the employee base, but also the bottom-line value of the fundamental obligation to ensure fair, honest, transparent, and authentic representation to all stakeholders, from employees and customers to vendors, investors, and the communities they serve.

Although the practice of diversity within corporate America has gained traction, the greatest challenge ahead lies with equity and inclusion. Companies must first understand the distinction between equity and equality, and then take measurable, visible, intentional steps with inclusion at all levels. This begins by asking some very basic questions, not as a one-time exercise, but ongoing throughout the lifespan of the company. Are we hearing from all voices regarding our most pressing initiatives? What are we doing to be inclusive? Is the diversity of our workforce reflective of our customer base? Does our leadership represent the diverse insights and perspectives of our employees and other stakeholders? What are we doing to improve our brand, image, and footprint as a leader in DEI?

Companies that undergo an honest assessment of their DEI efforts and an audit of their opportunities in this area position themselves to have better outcomes with their DEI initiatives in the long term. Authenticity is key in making change, and organizations should know that stakeholders can recognize when DEI efforts are half-hearted or short-lived.

Consider the company that, as part of its DEI initiatives, has created special employee groups (SEGs) as a way of creating a forum for employees to connect and communicate about internal issues. The women's group might discuss equal pay or work-life balance. The LGBTQ+ group might talk about earning a promotion or having their voice heard within other work settings. The African American group might discuss representation in the C-suite or the company's outreach to non-represented communities. Whatever the scenario, often, someone from leadership is there as the "sponsor" or executive team representative.

Sometimes, the company brings in a speaker who is African American to talk to the African American group, a high-profile woman leader to speak to that group, and so forth. After the meeting, everybody goes back to their office and feels great because they had a chance to have the conversation. In some cases, many people leave feeling as if nothing at the meeting really made a difference. No progress was made, no changes decided on, no part of the real conversation about inclusion was addressed. The results of these types of meetings are often minuscule, short-lived, and therefore meaningless. Perhaps the leadership approves more paid family leave under certain circumstances for certain employees. Maybe the HR department is instructed to allow employees a certain number of paid hours to perform community service on behalf of the company. These "fixes" sound good on the surface, but are, in fact, only minor efforts to appease people and check the DEI box.

DIVERSITY BY DESIGN

Companies that want to lead in the DEI space must be transparent and over-communicate. Invite an open dialogue to discuss issues people are thinking about, but about which they may not express their thoughts. Avoiding difficult conversations about race, sexual orientation, or ageism, for example, can lead to passive aggressive behavior.

This new era of business is making space for people to openly express their authentic selves. Smart corporations will welcome that expression and find ways to integrate it into the corporate culture. Everyone has knowledge, experience, and perspectives that are different and valuable. Respecting people's lived experiences without being threatened by them makes us all better. Build a culture that embraces DEI. Don't just talk it when it's convenient.

Consider the scenario when the executive team decides to host a Cinco de Mayo celebration because a third of the employees are Hispanic. They order Mexican food and decorate the office with the colors of Mexico. The event they thought would bring people together actually becomes patronizing because it is filled with many of the stereotypes often connected to a group. Instead of having a conversation that seeks to understand, and making meaningful progress toward equity and inclusion, the company creates an enormous chasm between those in the majority and others at the company who seek to be seen, included, and valued. What is missing, is the unification of people, an understanding that every voice has equal value, and an authentic welcoming of everyone to the table.

Corporate America should feel a sense of urgency in making real change in DEI because the very survival of companies depends on it. As this millennium progresses, the continued upward trajectory of every corporation will, in fact, rest on its people. Companies that choose to embrace this new era of DEI will be rewarded in the form of enhanced performance indicators, such as production, employee satisfaction and longevity, customer loyalty, stock price, brand adoption, and increased revenues. Those who choose to ignore the DEI landscape will do so at their peril. In this competitive marketplace, DEI should be viewed not as a handout or as making up for previous wrongs, but as a strategic imperative for remaining competitive. This new era of DEI is more vital than ever to the progress, productivity, and profitability of corporations.

Lead

Prior to me taking on my new role as President and CEO of the Houston Hispanic Chamber of Commerce, the *Houston Business Journal* ranked the Chamber last place in its list of twenty-five chambers of commerce in the city of Houston. The only place we could go on that list was up, and we did. A few years later, the *HBJ* moved us from twenty-fifth in the ranking to second place, surpassed only by the Greater Houston Partnership, a testament to our commitment to be the best chamber of commerce in the region.

The board and I agreed that my top priority as the new leader of the organization was to work with them to restructure the bylaws and governance. Our objective was to set a new foundation and to move forward with a ten-year strategic plan, a unified agenda that allowed us to work with urgency with specific goals to set us apart from other chambers and similar organizations. Stepping into the leadership role of an organization poised for a change was a welcome challenge for me, one I was prepared to face with every ounce of passion and persistence within me. I took the job, not because of what the Chamber was, but because of what I visualized it could be. I knew it had the potential to be a force in Houston and beyond. That could only be accomplished with a collective effort by board members and staff.

The start of my journey at the Chamber was challenging in many ways because we chose to assess everything within the context of Houston's broader business community and by being more determined, more focused, and more intentional. To be a successful organization, we needed to have a clear brand and we had to build a marketing presence upon that brand. I saw the Chamber as a credible, reliable authority for the media on mainstream topics, such as energy, jobs, immigration, housing, and education, a voice of Hispanic business, and a source of pride for the Hispanic community and for Houstonians as a whole. Our success was achieved through a concerted effort to deliver high-level, well-executed programs elevating the profile and the perception of Hispanic businesses, which had the added benefit of positioning us as a beacon of promise for the Hispanic community in Houston, in Texas, and throughout the United States.

I knew from the beginning that we had to walk the talk of diversity, equity, and inclusion by broadening our reach to new business sectors and by welcoming non-Hispanics to our table and engaging with them. No longer could we remain in a silo if we wanted to reach the next level. Every day was an opportunity to add influence to the work we were doing by building relationships with prominent, influential leaders who knew nothing about the Hispanic Chamber and by understanding that the end game was to serve small businesses through changing perceptions. That kind of change required a lot of hard work, almost to the point of stopping everything the Chamber had previously done and starting anew. We were constantly looking for new ways to maintain a high bar of professionalism for the organization. The pace was accelerated in the early years because I was working with urgency, but that pace was necessary to elevate the organization to a level of prominence that the board and I envisioned.

Equally important was positioning the Chamber as an essential part of the future by impacting young professionals. Through a concerted effort with our board and staff, we created the Greater Houston Hispanic Chamber of Commerce Foundation with a specific goal in mind, to establish an elite professional development program, which we later named the Emerging Leaders Institute. Today, that program boasts more than three hundred graduates who have gone on to run for elective office, hold leadership positions in companies, start their own businesses, and influence their peers and others. In his book, *Prophetic City: Houston on the Cusp of a Changing America* (Klineberg 2020), Dr. Stephen L. Klineberg states, "Dr. Laura Murillo has developed programs for cultivating future leaders that may well have a long-term impact on Houston. … Houston is on the cusp of a changing America."

With this program and more to come, I saw the Chamber as not only an ethnic organization, but as one that could be, as new our tagline stated, "The Leader of Houston's New Majority." As much as I heard about the naysayers who rejected our positioning and ignored our value, I was even more aware that there were people cheering us on, expecting us to succeed, and willing to support us on the road to success.

When we announced the new slogan to the media, I received a phone call from a prominent journalist in Houston, who was compelled to share his words of disagreement that we had adopted such a tagline. He spent at least ten minutes yelling and screaming at me over the phone, using vulgar language about how racist the Chamber was to even consider such a statement. "I can't believe the board could be so arrogant as to proclaim the chamber as the leader of the new majority."

As I listened calmly to his ranting, I could hear the anger in his voice. From my perspective, his words were the expression of fear, of someone concerned that something that belonged to him was being threatened. Someone with his position in the media should have known better than to confront me with such vile incivility. Clearly, he was insulted that the Hispanic community, represented by the Chamber of Commerce, had the audacity to express a truth that we believed for ourselves, simply that we had a place in the city and in society, that we valued ourselves and our communities. Our proclamation had nothing to do with taking down anyone else. It was merely our declaration that we would speak for ourselves, rather than have others speak for us. We were simply and honestly asserting that we were owning our future and destiny and wrapping ourselves around the idea that we could resolve challenges and put forth a plan to excel.

With his rant coming to an end, he realized I was not engaging with him. That was my strategy. In all honesty, his unfounded dismay let me know we were succeeding; we were making progress. My simple statement to him was: "I'm sorry you feel this way. I appreciate you calling me. We stand by our statement as the leader of Houston's New Majority." With that, he hung up.

Despite that unfortunate encounter, the Chamber kept executing our goals and building the brand, rising as a force to be reckoned with among the Hispanic community as well as the broader business community in Houston and beyond. We also remained focused on growing our own diversity within the organization. Eventually, forty percent of our board members were non-Hispanic. That was important because we needed to be the example of diversity, equity, and inclusion, a focal point of our platform. Over the course of several years, I invited the prominent journalist to several events and emailed him about our successes. I chose the high road to show examples of the positive impact the Chamber was making on the city of Houston.

Eventually, he came to see the great work we were doing and understood that our efforts to establish our place in the world didn't mean his place was threatened. His rant was part of a fear that many people experience when they see the world changing. Disruption seems like a threat to what traditionalists hold dear. I have always sought to demonstrate that diversity isn't an "us vs. you" proposition; it's an "all of us together" perspective. I had to show the journalist that what we were doing would benefit the entire state and beyond, in every sector. What he had to learn over time is that inclusion for one does not equate to the exclusion of others. When we work together and respect each other as equals, everyone wins. That experience taught me to focus on goals and supporters and to not be distracted by those who choose to undermine or discourage me with negativity. Time and again, the opportunity to learn that important life lesson has presented itself.

Several years after that incident, I decided to run a 5K marathon as a personal challenge. Although not an athlete by any means, I counted on my daily fully packed schedule to prepare me for the endeavor. When the race began, I ran as fast as I could with the excitement of challenging myself physically and reaching the finish line. The hundreds of people who lined the streets cheered on all the runners. "Go, go, go! You got this," they yelled, as I ran through the streets. As I turned the corner, I noticed two men standing off to the side. "Look at her!" one yelled.

"She's so slow." Not until then did I realized that most of the other runners had already passed me, and the race had just begun.

Immediately, I doubted my ability to complete the race because of what those two men had said about me. The facts told the story. Yes, I was slower than most as I rounded the curve, but what I realized in that moment was that my goal was to finish the race. Period. Not to finish first. In a flash, I changed my strategy. My daily routine of going from one meeting to the next had taught me that I was a faster walker than a runner. Why try to keep up with the others in the race? I wasn't there for them. This was a personal goal that I had to achieve my way. Then, I thought of my daughters. Our family mantra began to play in my mind, "You are smart, you are beautiful, and God loves you." That meditation, along with the cheers, and not the jeers, allowed me to finish what I started, something I practice at every opportunity as I lead in life.

Bucket list. Finishing my first 5K run. I learned that I could walk faster than I could run.

Diversity Champions

I have never let money stand in the way of achieving my goals. Focusing on money, or the lack thereof, can be an obstacle to growth and visibility for an organization. Remaining focused on the outcome and the impact I hope to make, I figure out the money piece as I go along. Knowing that, I will find ways to engage others to support my goals. My approach has been to visualize what I want to accomplish, add value for others, and sell my ideas with passion and persistence. Invariably, the money comes, the partnerships come, the negotiating happens, in-kind exchanges of services takes place, and the collaboration occurs.

A few months after I took the helm, we learned the lease on our office space had expired, and we had to find a new home for the Chamber. Several board members and I shopped around all of Houston for the ideal office space for what was shaping up to be the new and improved Chamber. We ran into a lot of noes, until Paul Murphy, then President of Amegy Bank of Texas, gave us a yes. Amegy Bank paid for the build-out of the Chamber's new space, and we assured Paul that Amegy would benefit from having us in their building.

When we set up the meeting with Paul to discuss the office space in Amegy's downtown building, we went in knowing we wanted to build a long-term relationship with both Paul and with Amegy Bank. That morning in his office, we spoke candidly with him. "Paul, we need office space, and if we are headquartered in your building, we can provide your bankers with direct access to small business owners." He quietly heard us out. "The Chamber doesn't have any money, Paul, but what we do have are board members and supporters who will move their deposits over to Amegy." We wanted him to see the win-win in our proposition.

> **LEAD IN LIFE MOMENT**
>
> Don't go into a negotiation with your vision only. Think about how the other side will benefit. They need to know what's in it for them and how your proposition will help with their objectives. Know the other person's goals and be ready to communicate clearly how you can help them.

Paul understood our message, and Amegy Bank donated a generous space in its building for the Chamber's offices, with a multi-year renewal contract, and agreed to fund the entire cost of building out the space with the grandeur we had envisioned as the new image for the Chamber. From there, our relationship with Amegy Bank blossomed.

Approximately two years after the initial meeting with Paul, I went back, this time to ask for larger office space on another floor of the building. I felt confident doing this because we had built a solid relationship and I knew the Chamber had become a valued resource for him. Because I had been keeping him posted on the Chamber's progress and successes, I didn't have to convince him about our need for more space. At every step, where appropriate, I held to the promise of championing Amegy and encouraging our constituents to utilize their services. That ask was met with Paul's nearly immediate acceptance, and the opportunities for the Chamber's expansion continued.

Over the years, Paul and I met frequently and shared introductions among colleagues with mutually beneficial outcomes. One afternoon, we were scheduled for a one-on-one to discuss further collaborations. When I walked into his office, Paul smiled and said, "Hello. What can I do for you, Laura Murillo?" It was as if he knew in advance that I was there for something specific. I requested the use of the entire eleventh floor of the Amegy building, which was not being utilized at that time, but had previously served as an event space for up to 350 people. I suggested that Paul allow us to use the space to hold an event launching our ten-year strategic plan. In exchange, we would provide Amegy with branding, media exposure, and access to our board, VIPs, elected officials, and others. Again, Paul agreed. A couple of years later, that space was leased out and we lost access to it.

Ever observant, I noticed, several times a week, Amegy Bank staff would leave our downtown building for training at Amegy's headquarter offices in the Galleria. What I saw as an inconvenience for their staff sparked an idea for me that I had to present to Paul. Why not build out a new conference and training center for his employees located in the downtown Amegy building where we were located? While the space would be used by Amegy, the Chamber could also use it to provide seminars to our members at no cost to the Chamber.

"Let me get this right," he said. "You think I need a conference center at the downtown Amegy Bank building, which conveniently, the Chamber will also be able to use?"

"Yes, that's exactly what I'm saying."

Always the champion of diversity, Paul agreed. Even after my numerous requests of Paul over the years, he was always able to see the mutual benefits of all my requests.

In 2021, I had one more big ask of Paul, and that was to consider serving as the chairman of our board of directors. He would become the first white male to serve in that role, a testament to my efforts to diversify the Chamber's board and to Paul's belief in where we were headed. He agreed, and the board voted unanimously in favor of him as chairman. Once again, we doubled down our diversity objectives and set ourselves up for a bright future in Houston's business arena.

———————— ● ————————

The Hispanic population in Houston grew exponentially in the 2000s and our voices needed to be heard. The Chamber had helped to enlighten the general business population about what Hispanic businesses could offer and the economic impact we were making and could make on our city. My internal motto was: "As Hispanics go, so goes Houston." Still, I knew it wasn't about us; it was about we. When we, as Hispanics, do well, so does Houston. With that perspective, I began holding press conferences on comprehensive immigration, strategies to bring more businesses to Houston, a collaborative approach to economic development, and the grave necessity for corporations to implement meaningful diversity, equity, and inclusion practices. Suddenly, the media began to come to me and ask for comment on important topics. The plan for the new Chamber was taking form.

Advocacy and press conferences, with diverse participants, became a focal point for us early in my tenure. Also, we made a concerted effort to write white papers and op-eds and to continue to position ourselves as "The Leader of Houston's New Majority." Eventually, we began working with Vinson & Elkins law firm, where I had a longstanding relationship with Beto Cardenas and Harry Reasoner. Some of the Chamber's primary advocacy items included NAFTA (USMCA), voting engagement, comprehensive immigration reform, and DACA (Deferred Action for Childhood Arrivals). We could do only so much advocating on our own, so it was definitely strategic to partner with Vinson & Elkins and establish an opportunity to voice our support for individuals brought to the U.S. as children by their parents.

Advocating on behalf of DACA recipients and in support of comprehensive immigration reform. Joined by Houston's fearless leaders for a press conference at City Hall.

Hundreds of thousands of children and young adults in Houston were in jeopardy of being deported. The partnership became a $750,000 in-kind investment of legal services that grew into other opportunities for the law firm and for the Chamber. The Chamber had never done that type of in-kind partnership before. I was tasked with getting people to sign on in support of DACA, and the Chamber took a bold and significant step by filing the amicus brief related to DACA. The difference between advocating for the Chamber through the media and making bold moves on policy through legal channels took us into the major league.

As our visibility grew, we worked closely with sports teams, including the Astros, the Texans, and others, to secure in-kind sponsorship from them where it was mutually beneficial. Jamey Rootes, then president of the Houston Texans, was the first to agree to exchange private suites and other sponsor deliverables, including advertising in their programs, videos of the Chamber shown during the games, and prime space on their website. Our platform grew exponentially within two years, and the Chamber was named Regional and National Chamber of the Year by the U.S. Hispanic Chamber of Commerce for the remarkable transformation. The recognition increased the Chamber's national presence, not only among our peers, but also among local and national corporate sponsors. Additionally, the American Marketing Association acknowledged us with Marketer of the Year for three years. The year our logo was redesigned, the Chamber beat out several other organizations, including the Houston Super Bowl Committee, even though their marketing budget was significantly larger.

Always hoping to inspire the next generation of leaders, I personally invited a delegation of young leaders to join me at local, state, and national conferences. The first Emerging Leaders cohort joined me at the United States Hispanic Chamber of Commerce conference. Most chambers arrived with one or two staff or board members. We arrived with more than thirty emerging leaders dressed professionally. I positioned them throughout the room to network with prominent business leaders from across the country, making an indelible impression on everyone in attendance. Their presence was about more than just exposing young people to the business arena. It was about demonstrating the Houston Hispanic Chamber's dedication to diversity.

The next step was to expand the Chamber's visibility by finding a media platform. I realized the numerous events we hosted, such as the annual luncheon, our fundraising gala, a health summit, the women's conference, the business institute, and receptions for elected officials, were opportunities to recruit board members from various business sectors. The media platform would not only make a huge impact on the Chamber's membership numbers, but it would also boost our visibility to the non-Hispanic population, a vital part of the vision for the organization. In addition to the other efforts, we understood the importance of securing a visible media platform, something no other chamber was doing, and how it would set us apart from other nonprofits. I also knew the enormous amount of time, work, and effort would be required to serve as the founding executive producer and host of all these television and radio programs.

A list was made of top media outlets in Houston, and I pitched the idea of a television program that would spotlight success stories of entrepreneurs and executives. Unfortunately, no one was interested. Some of the mainstream stations suggested I go to the Spanish stations. Although that was part of my long-term plan, I wanted my initial entry into the world of media to be through the mainstream stations. I revised my approach to focus more on demographic data and what could be done for the station in terms of bringing in an audience and building loyalty.

Susan McEldoon, President and General Manager of KHOU-11, the local CBS affiliate, was open to the idea because we had cultivated a strong relationship. "As long as you can produce the show and just give us the tape, we will air it," she said. That was the start of our TV program and the start of our media impact on the city of Houston. One of our first guests was our sitting governor, Rick Perry. Getting him as a guest didn't just happen; it required persistence on my part.

After months of calling the governor's office and sharing information with his team about the reach and value of our viewing audience, and the benefits of having that audience see him on our program, I finally received confirmation that he would do the interview. That day, several of our staff gathered in my office to listen in on the conversation. The governor's staff person confirmed the details of the interview and asked me if we had a makeup artist. Without skipping a beat, I replied that we indeed had someone who could do Governor Perry's makeup prior to the show. At the conclusion of the call, I noticed the surprised faces of the staff. They were excited about the governor's confirmation, but even more appalled at my indication that we had a makeup artist.

Rosie Martinez, VP at the chamber, said, "We don't have a makeup artist, Dr. Murillo."

Always one to set the stage and figure out the rest, I glanced at Rosie and asked, "You wear makeup every day, don't you, Rosie?" With a curious look on her face, she replied in the affirmative. I then said, "Okay, take twenty dollars from petty cash, go to the dollar store, buy some powder, a powder brush, and to look professional, be sure to buy a plastic cape to place around his suit."

Demonstrating quick, strategic thinking was my way of teaching and developing the staff, helping them understand that where there's a will, there's always a way. Did Governor Perry have a clue that his makeup artist wasn't a trained professional? Probably not. But we got the job done and the interview was a success. We made a positive impression on the governor of Texas and our audience saw that the Houston Hispanic Chamber had the influence to attract high-level leaders throughout the state.

CBS KHOU 11 interview with Texas Governor Rick Perry regarding economic development.

———•———

Thanks to Sarah Frazier, vice president of CBS Radio, a radio program on CBS was secured and aired on six of their top stations in Houston with an audience reach of more than three million. On this radio program, I interviewed CEOs, elected officials, and Houston's top business leaders.

One day, I received a call from Joe Lopez, the public relations representative for Ford Motor Vehicles. He and I had known each other for decades, and he understood how different the Houston Hispanic Chamber of Commerce was from other chambers of commerce across the country. Ford had secured about a thirty-minute Spanish-language radio program on Univision, and Joe invite me to be founding executive producer and host of the program. I jumped at the chance. The challenge was that the show was to begin in just two days.

"Can you put something together that quickly?" he asked.

"Of course, I can."

Without even knowing what I would do, I accepted the challenge, and worked with urgency to pull together content for the new Spanish-radio program. Clearly, our first show would not have a guest because we had too short notice to send invitations. Plus, it was more important to set the stage for this new program, which would catapult the Chamber's visibility among the Spanish-speaking population.

With no script, I spoke for thirty minutes from my heart, drawing upon anecdotes to convey my message, offering words of motivation about how everyone has an opportunity to do something with their life, to take advantage of each day, and to be grateful. The message was that we all provide value, and although we face challenges, we have to find ways to seek support and to serve others with our talents. The show went off without a hitch, and I was proud that we were able to pull something together so quickly. The Ford Motor Company was pleased.

A few weeks after that first show aired, a woman visited the Chamber's office and asked to speak to me. She had taken the METRO train from the Memorial area of Houston, where she was a nanny. Unfortunately, I was out of the office, on my way to deliver a keynote speech about demographics to an audience of city employees and elected officials in Conroe, Texas. Right before I stepped into City Hall, I received a call from my office. The staffer told me a woman was at the Chamber office and wished to speak with me.

In Spanish, she said, "I want to thank you for coming into my life through the radio program. I heard you speak, and your words touched me so much."

The woman had been in a very dark place for some time and had considered taking her life. Both she and her daughter were victims of domestic violence, and when she heard my voice, she said she felt as if I was speaking to her. It meant so much to know my words touched this woman so deeply and had such a positive impact on her that she came across town to thank me. "You were an angel to me," she said. "You saved my life." If no other outcome had resulted from that radio show on Univision, I would have been satisfied with that. Her sincere words let me know what we were doing was needed and appreciated.

Soon after, thanks to my relationship with Craig Bland, Vice President and General Manager of Univision, we secured a Spanish-language radio and television program on Univision and UniMás, where I would be the founding executive producer and host. The topics were resource-oriented, with information to help individuals understand how to get a GED, the importance of voting, where to take courses to learn English, resources for becoming a citizen, and more.

In 2018, I decided it was important to showcase Houston's elite power players. I awoke at three o'clock in the morning, excited with the name of the next television program. It would be called *Houston Legends* and would air on the KUBE-57, where I served as founding executive producer and host. This show would include fifteen-minute interviews with local business leaders, such as Phoebe Tudor; Shelby Hodge; Tony Chase, Tilman Fertitta; former Mayor of Houston Annise Parker; Neil Bush; Ellen Ochoa, the first Hispanic woman astronaut to go to space; Judge Lina Hidalgo, the first Hispanic woman elected Harris County Judge; Harris County Commissioner Adrian Garcia; and Mary Bass. In addition to establishing the media platform, I wanted to insert the Chamber into the mainstream mindset.

We also partnered with the *Houston Chronicle*, the *Houston Business Journal*, Houston Public Media-NPR, and Clear Channel Media to secure full-page ads, public service announcements, and billboards prominently displayed across the city and showing only the new Chamber logo and our $54 million local economic impact.

The value of these and so many other in-kind services during my fifteen-year tenure as president and CEO has exceeded $20 million. This enormous investment expanded the brand and visibility of the Chamber and provided valuable resources and information to the broader Houston region. The impact on the diverse audiences reached and the caliber of the guests helped the Chamber step out of the silo of being viewed in the light of reaching only a Hispanic audience.

———— ● ————

The devastation from Hurricane Ike in 2008 included hundreds of lives lost nationwide, more than one hundred dead in Houston alone, and billions of dollars in damages. When Mayor Bill White asked me to serve on the Hurricane Ike Recovery Committee, I quickly accepted and set out to learn of the areas most affected by the storm and what their immediate needs were.

Mayor Bill White and Doug Hall asked me to join them backstage to collect a $250,000 donation from singer, Neil Diamond. The next day, Diamond asked to meet with me privately and I was able to secure $5 million from him for Hurricane Ike victims.

Part of my role on the committee was to manage the influx of large donations to the area, one of which came from a friend of Houston, award-winning musical performer, Neil Diamond. Houston was one of the first cities that welcomed him as a budding star in the early days of his decades-long career and had remained dear to his heart. When the mayor called my office to invite me to join him backstage at Neil Diamond's concert to accept a $250,000 donation, my answer was a hearty and immediate yes. In my heart of hearts, however, I knew the possibility existed that more could be done to help those devastated by the storm.

Backstage with Neil Diamond and Mayor White, I took the brief opportunity to share with Mr. Diamond some facts I believed would provide a broader perspective of the severity of the situation. I explained that the town of Anahuac, less than fifty miles outside of Houston, was one of the most affected areas. People there had been killed in their own homes, bodies from other areas were seen floating through the small town, and the majority of families had lost their homes. "Thank you for your investment in helping to rebuild those lives," I said. With that, Mr. Diamond shook my hand and we left.

The next day, a call came into the Chamber office from someone identifying himself as Neil Diamond. When my staff put the call through to me, I was sure it was a joke, but when I heard the voice, I was convinced. "Hello, this is Neil Diamond. We met last night, and I would like to come over to your office today to continue our conversation."

I agreed and immediately went into preparation mode, reaching out to inform the mayor and the chairman of the Hurricane Ike Recovery Committee, Albert Meyers, to ensure I was practicing proper protocol. Sure enough, Neil Diamond arrived at our offices, clad in a Members Only jacket, a baseball cap, and shades, along with his manager, a burly gentleman who seemed less than pleased with the impromptu meeting.

Mr. Diamond arrived at my office around four o'clock in the afternoon, took a seat across from me, and said, "I read about you, Dr. Murillo, and all the work you've done in Houston. I can tell you're a woman with a big heart. Please tell me more about what's going on with the people in Houston and what I can do to help them recover from this travesty." His sincerity was undeniable.

As I explained more about the city's recovery efforts and needs, specifically the destruction and loss of life in Anahuac, I could see his manager getting anxious. He eventually interrupted to remind Mr. Diamond that he had an appearance in Dallas and his plane was prepared to depart soon. Unfazed, Mr. Diamond instructed me to continue, reminding the manager that he owned the plane and it would leave whenever he was ready.

With that, I invited Mr. Diamond to drive with me to Anahuac that afternoon so he could see the devastation for himself. He agreed. What had slipped my mind in the moment was that I too had an engagement that very evening. I was scheduled to receive an award at 6:30 at the BBVA soccer stadium. With my heart and mind focused on helping those in need, and the chance to illustrate that dire need in a most direct way to someone who could have a huge impact, my "work with urgency" mode kicked in.

"Mr. Diamond, do you mind if I invite our committee chairman, Mr. Meyers, to join us?" I asked.

With a bit of hesitancy, he said, "Sure, but keep in mind that I want to talk to *you*. You know what I'm trying to do, and you're going to be my spokesperson. By the way," he added, "please call me Neil." I agreed and within ten minutes we departed my office with Neil Diamond, Mr. Meyers, and the manager.

On the drive to Anahuac, I called the mayor of the town to inform him that we would be arriving soon with a celebrity and that no media or photographers should be invited. This visit wasn't a photo opportunity; it was the sincere gesture of a concerned citizen who could help the residents of this town recover. Less than an hour later, we arrived and drove around the town, noting blue tarps that draped dilapidated structures, once homes to the people who had lost everything. A small group of people gathered outside a church, huddled in prayer for their town and the lives lost. They shared granola bars, small bottles of water, and other snacks that they'd pulled together. I explained to Neil that FEMA had not yet arrived to offer help.

"Oh, Dr. Laura, what should I do?" he asked.

Without a second thought, I said, "We need to stop. We need to get out and just listen to them."

We approached the group, who sat in folding chairs discussing the devastation their town had experienced and how they would begin to get back on their feet. A few feet away, I noticed a woman staring at me, her eyes asking, "Is that Neil Diamond?" We locked eyes and I slowly nodded my head to acknowledge her, and then I whispered to Neil, "I think you've been spotted. What do you want to do?"

With a tinge of concern in his voice, he replied, "What do you want me to do?"

To ease the pressure for him to act, I stood and introduced myself to the group. "We're sorry to interfere with your meeting. I want to let you know that Mr. Neil Diamond is here, and last night, he invested $250,000 to the recovery effort." The crowd gasped as I continued. "I told him about the devastation your community has gone through, and he wanted to come here himself to offer his condolences." They all began to cry.

One woman stepped forward and said, "We appreciate you coming. No one else has come to see us. We feel like cockroaches."

Neil listened ardently to each person, their concerns, and their stories. I could tell he was touched by their impassioned accounts.

Nearly in tears, Neil said, "I'm so sorry you guys went through this. I'm here because of this woman right here. She has a big heart. She spoke for you. She told me I had to come and meet you, and I'm glad I did. When I started as a singer, I was being booked in little bitty crap-holes around New York. Houston was the first place that booked me for a concert and embraced me and validated me as a singer," he shared. They all listened and received the sincerity of his words and concern.

After a few minutes, Neil thanked them for sharing their stories, and he hugged every person there, and then we bade them farewell. The impact of that engagement on Neil Diamond was undeniable. As we drove away, Neil looked to me and said, "Doctor, I feel so grateful. You've touched my heart. Can I take you and Mr. Meyers to grab something to eat? I don't want any attention. I just want to talk to you guys."

By then, I had called the Chamber offices to advise my staff that I would not be able to make the awards ceremony at the soccer stadium, so I was more than happy to join Neil and the others for dinner at Ninfa's Mexican Restaurant. Neil insisted he didn't want to be a distraction at the restaurant, and since I knew the restaurant's manager, I asked him to discretely walk us to a private table in the back. As we entered and walked through the restaurant, several of the patrons and staff waved hello and greeted me. "Hey, Dr. Laura, good to see you!" they said, as we passed through. "Well, that's embarrassing," Neil said. "Here I was thinking I was the star and looks like you're the one who is the star, my dear."

Over a delicious meal, we talked about Neil's music and how he wrote his hit song "Sweet Caroline." Prior to ordering our food, Neil's manager informed me that Neil was on a restricted diet, which included no alcohol, no sugar, and no starch. Immediately, I knew Neil would love the special combination plate with a chicken enchilada, beef taco, rice, and beans. To top it off, I ordered him a margarita with no ice. His manager looked at me in disbelief, but to his surprise, Neil indulged in it all and said it was the best meal he'd had in ages.

As our dinner came to a close, Neil leaned over and whispered to me that he had decided to increase his $250,000 donation to $5 million. I was so filled with gratitude at his generosity and sincere concern for the people of Anahuac and Houston.

On the drive back to the city, Neil said, "Thank you for living this day with me and thank you for all you do. This was one of the best days of my life." Then, he reached over and took my hand in his. "Now, we must part ways because today I broke all of my dietary restrictions and spent $5 million after meeting you for just ten minutes yesterday."

Neil Diamond asked me to speak on his behalf during an impromptu visit to Anahuac, Texas, where we met with Hurricane Ike victims.

I suggested that Neil Diamond join me to visit Anahuac, TX, to witness the catastrophic impact of Hurricane Ike.

Become a Connector

Throughout my career journey at the University of Houston, Memorial Hermann, and particularly in my role as president and CEO of the Houston Hispanic Chamber of Commerce, I have developed an insight into diversity, equity, and inclusion that draws upon my personal background and professional experience of being "the first," "the youngest," or "the only one" with a seat at the decision-making table.

Informally at first, and then quite intentionally as my career progressed, I took notice of opportunities that organizations missed to become more diverse and stand out as champions of inclusion for the betterment of those they serve and represent. Similarly, holding a seat at the coveted decision-making table many times, I have noted where equity practices were absent and when the concept of inclusion was simply not considered. These situations have caused me to be a relentless connector, unstoppable in my efforts to make critical connections in every situation, particularly when the opportunity arises to introduce influencers to talented women and minorities.

My lived experiences as a Latina, a woman, a daughter of immigrants, and a single mom have informed me about the sometimes-subtle distinctions that keep organizations from being more inclusive and some of the obvious concerns that prevent minority organizations from inviting and welcoming support from outsiders. Diversity and inclusion work both ways. There should always be a way in for those who don't look like the majority of faces in the room, whether at an all-white board meeting, in an all-female organization, in a room full of straight professionals, or where fifty-plus is the average age.

As I took note of my experiences as a rising professional with a growing list of A-rated contacts, influencers, and prominent individuals in various business sectors, I began advocating for those who had not been welcomed to the table in corporate settings, on boards, and in the C-suite. These were extremely intelligent, insightful, highly educated, accomplished, and personable individuals who might look like me but weren't invited in, not because they were not qualified, but because they didn't have the same contacts I had. They were, in fact, among the best of the best, who happened to be women or minorities. My responsibility has been to make introductions so that, as the organizations I know seek to embrace DEI, they have the resources to act on their goals.

Now, whenever I hear of a key opportunity that one of my corporate contacts is presenting, such as a job opening or a contract bid request, I recommend a candidate or consult my contact list to make an introduction. Whenever I do, and the outcome is favorable, I receive calls thanking me for making the introduction that resulted in a new hire, a new job, a promotion, a board seat, an interview, or something else beneficial for each person. When I first began doing this, it was just a natural thing for me because I'm a connector by nature. I had no idea that what I saw as a small gesture—a simple introduction that became a connection—could matter so much to so many. Those connections are vital to the future progress of others' careers, just as similar connections have been for me.

At many times throughout my career, whenever I made the decision to embark on a new endeavor, I sought out someone who had already done it. Seeing that someone else has accomplished what I want to do is a motivator, especially if that person is like me, female, Hispanic, and of a similar age. They inspire me. The same is likely true for others within any organization that supports the value of having a diverse workforce at every level of an organization. If no one else looks like me in the space where I seek to be, my dream seems more remote, more difficult to attain. Unfortunately, in the realm of corporate and organizational diversity, women and minorities are not at the table in large enough numbers to have an honest, transparent, and effective conversation that leads to change. I seek to remedy that for those in my circle of influence.

In my daily interactions with CEOs, I have regularly heard them say, "Dr. Murillo, you're so accomplished. Your bio is so impressive. I wish we could find someone like you to fill this position." Although I appreciate their comments, I want them to know there are many accomplished professionals like me who exceed the qualifications for the position and who also bring extensive insights to expand the company's perspective and reach key audiences. In these instances, I reply, "Tell me

LEAD IN LIFE MOMENT

Don't go into a negotiation with your vision only. Think about how the other side will benefit. They need to know what's in it for them and how your proposition will help with their objectives. Know the other person's goals and be ready to communicate clearly how you can help them.

what you need," certain that I know at least one person I can connect with them who meets the qualifications. My goal is to listen, understand, and provide a solution.

I also enjoy helping others who have been stuck in their career and are ready for their next step. Connecting candidates with opportunities brings me such joy because each of these contacts are highly educated and have vast experience, but simply might have no other way to connect with the opportunities. Those in leadership positions often have no idea how frustrating it can be for qualified people to meet with one roadblock after another when seeking to go higher in their career. I encourage those I know to send me their information and keep doing their part to build visibility by speaking on panels, submitting their name for board seats, applying for new job opportunities, and making themselves available for media opportunities as an expert resource.

LEAD IN LIFE MOMENT

When building your brand, control what you can—your actions, your words, your presentation. You do this one person, one experience at a time. Every action and experience adds to the composite leading to your end game. Do what you say you'll do. Over-deliver. Remember that you are building your reputation as you build your brand.

Whenever I learn of a new opportunity, my go-to group of professionals is the more than three hundred graduates of the Chamber's Emerging Leaders Program, an elite group of very capable next-generation leaders who exude confidence and stand ready to respond to opportunities I share with them. Just as my mentors have helped me by putting me in the spotlight, I gain great pleasure in doing the same for them.

DEI: Make it Matter

While the Chamber continued its efforts to elevate Houston's entire Hispanic community by becoming part of the mainstream conversation, I connected with the media and other experts on a variety of topics, which invariably included DEI insights in some form. Because of my extensive outreach and strong messaging, the media began to contact me to comment on DEI and other topics, and I consistently received speaking invitations, nationally and internationally, to be a guest speaker on topics related to DEI and other critical business matters.

I developed a DEI strategy for the Chamber, which included partnering with firms such as McKinsey & Company, the UH Hobby School for Public Policy, Rice University, Korn Ferry, Spencer Stuart, the *Houston Chronicle*, the *Houston Business Journal,* and many others to share vital information on the new era of DEI, always thinking of how this would benefit their efforts to expand diversity. These organizations were already taking steps in this direction, but I brought my upbringing and my own experience of having a seat at a diverse table throughout my career to help accelerate the pace at which these initiatives were being adopted. One led to many, and my conversations with corporate leaders multiplied.

DIVERSITY BY DESIGN

The need for diversity exists in equal measure within woman-based or minority-based organizations. These groups also need to demonstrate diversity in hiring, in management, and on their boards. Decision-makers who influence the diversity of an organization should honestly examine the equity and inclusion practices to explore opportunities for improvement. In order for any organization to grow well into the twenty-first century, everyone can't look alike.

As President and CEO of the Houston Hispanic Chamber of Commerce, I had to walk the talk of DEI in order to make it matter in my presentations and remarks to the public. Therefore, I instituted an aggressive approach to our DEI initiative and changed the composition of the board of directors to include several non-Hispanics. Under my tenure, the Chamber board welcomed the first woman who was not Hispanic and the first non-Hispanic board chair and reached up to forty percent non-Hispanic composition for our board. I also encouraged the board to include non-Hispanics and those of various age groups in our Business Institute and our Emerging Leaders Institute.

Companies and organizations like the Chamber, who are sincerely pursuing a strategic DEI position, need to ask themselves some critical questions, such as: How do we want to demonstrate our DEI strategy in the marketplace? What changes do we need to make to ensure DEI is a continual and perpetual part of corporate culture and operations? What do we need to do to see our employees, board of directors, and executive team reflect our vision and objectives as relates to DEI? These are just a few among many insightful questions to ask along the road to true DEI implementation.

Convincing leaders of the urgency of DEI can be difficult when they are used to business as usual. However, the adage, "If it ain't broke, don't fix it" doesn't work with DEI. The social and racial unrest experienced in 2020 were clear indications that the decades of ignoring DEI issues in the workplace and in society has had, and will continue to have, severe negative effects on the economy and the profitability of top companies globally. For those leaders who dispute this, I share facts that speak louder than words.

An article published on June 8, 2021 by ABCNews.com cites a study by the Alliance on Board Diversity and the consulting firm Deloitte which indicates that, following the social justice protests that swept the United States, corporate board diversification stagnated. Across the Fortune 500 firms, 82.5 percent of board directors are white, 56 percent of S&P 500 companies have all-white boards (as of November 2020), and white women held three new board seats for every new seat occupied by a woman from a racial minority since 2019. ("Study: Racial diversity stagnated on corporate boards," ABCnews.go.com, June 8, 2021). Presenting hard facts to the business community often gives leaders pause to consider needed improvements for their organizations and how best to execute their own DEI strategies.

Companies that demonstrate a pattern of elevating those who are not already at the table position themselves to attract top talent and top dollars from customers, partners, and supporters. A report by McKinsey & Company reveals that companies in the top quartile for gender diversity on executive teams were 25 percent more likely to have above-average profitability than companies in the fourth quartile—up from 21 percent in 2017 and 15 percent in 2014. Additionally, companies with more than 30 percent women executives were more likely to outperform companies where this percentage ranged from 10 to 30 percent ("Diversity Wins: How Inclusion Matters," McKinsey & Company, May 19, 2020). Indeed, the most diverse companies are likely to outperform their non-diverse competitors. Thankfully, things are changing, but not rapidly enough. There is still much work to be done for corporate America to see real, substantial, and lasting change in their DEI efforts.

Servant Leadership

Service is in my DNA. From my early teens I knew I liked helping people. Becoming affiliated with organizations and serving in leadership roles with a variety of nonprofit groups has been a foundational part of my career path. One of the first groups to make a significant impact on my civic involvement and leadership was LULAC, League of United Latin American Citizens. After seeing Johnny Mata, president and district director, on TV, I approached the organization and asked to volunteer as a media supporter. That volunteer position led me to get involved with Hispanic Women in Leadership, where I met Olga Soliz and Dr. Dorothy Caram. Both women were pioneers and certainly made significant contributions and lasting impact.

While in my early twenties, I became a member and the youngest person to serve as president of Hispanic Women in Leadership. I gravitated to this organization, not because of what it was but because of what I thought it could be. I saw that it needed an infusion of new people. When I spoke before the group to campaign as president, I knew the other candidates had a lot more experience than I had, but I also knew I brought a fresh perspective and energy that the organization needed. I showed up prepared and I looked the part. In my speech, I shared with them my vision for what the organization could become. I brought to the table a vision for the future with younger women and men as an opportunity to spark new ideas and build a foundation for the sustainability of the organization. Years later, I was inducted into the Hispanic Women in Leadership Hall of Fame.

All those positions were building blocks for my reputation of serving and my objective to always leave things better than they were when I arrived. I wanted to branch out and extend my civic engagement beyond the Latino organizations into areas where there were few Hispanics at the table. I knew I wanted to make an impact in other circles to prove myself and to be an example to others that Hispanics have a voice to contribute to the broader conversations in this country. Also, I believed that being able to navigate within diverse circles of power and influence was important in order to ultimately help those who are the least amongst us.

Throughout the years, I believe I have been most impactful through the multiple economic, and civic leadership positions I have assumed, including as one of ten leaders in the country appointed to the Washington, DC Federal Reserve Board of Governors, Community Advisory Committee. Reporting to the Board of Governors, we are involved in matters of public policy, from monetary policy, housing, employment, inflation, small business, child care, and immigration reform. Our recommendations are shared with the Board of Governors, who are appointed by the President of the United States and are approved by Congress.

The idea that the daughter of immigrant parents would one day serve organizations in these various capacities still amazes me. But when I consider my never-ending drive to work with urgency in everything I do, and my sincere gratitude for those who have helped pave the way for me, I give thanks to the universe for placing me in places where I can be of the most service to others.

Federal Reserve Board of Governors
appoints

Dr. Laura G. Murillo
President & CEO
Houston Hispanic Chamber of Commerce

to the
Community Advisory Council

Honored as the first Houstonian appointed to the Washington, DC Federal Reserve Community Advisory Council. The CAC makes national public policy recommendations and reports to the Board of Governors. They are appointed by the President of the United States and are approved by Congress.

CHAPTER 5

INTUITION

A Mother's Love

My mother and I were inseparable. We saw each other almost every day of my life. Although we lived only a few blocks from each other, we talked on the phone several times a day, and she traveled with my girls and me for each vacation. Always offering help and advice to me as a mother, she was a pivotal force in helping me raise my daughters.

As my mother got older, her health declined. I tried to be patient with the reality of her illness, hoping that the love of family would stave off death for just a little while. My siblings and I took turns as caregivers, making certain someone was always by her side so she would never be alone. Along with my family, I did what I could to make her as comfortable as possible, and yet, our family came to the obvious and very heart-wrenching conclusion that she was not getting better. As the days passed and her illness progressed, I developed an overwhelming need to be close to her, so I would visit her home multiple times daily. One thing I learned through the very sad experience of her death is to trust my instinct.

One cool October day in 2011, I decided to spend the night with her. With the girls safe at home, my mom and I enjoyed some of her favorite things, like snacking on popcorn, watching old movies in bed, and reminiscing about her childhood in Mexico. I knew how much she loved her garden, so I carefully escorted her outside and handed her a pair of scissors so she could clip what would become the last rose she would ever cut. This time, I put the rose in the vase for her. Throughout the night she was happy, even lucid, although a bit frail. She was in no pain, and I was so grateful that God blessed me to spend that last night of her life with her.

While sitting in bed, she reached over and placed her hand upon mine and said, "Laura, remember, I want to die at home."

"Of course, mom. Don't worry about that," I assured her as we lay there holding hands until she fell asleep.

At three o'clock in the morning, I suddenly awoke with an unexplainable urgency surging through my body. Instinctively, I knew my daughters, who were thirteen and ten years old at the time, needed to see their grandmother, and she needed to see them. Despite my fun-filled evening with my mother, I knew this could be the last time we would all be together. My mind told me this was the right thing to do, even though it meant I would wake up the girls so they could visit their grandmother in the wee hours of the morning.

I made arrangements for them to be driven over, and when they arrived at her house, I ushered them into her room. With midnight-colored skies peeking through the curtains in her bedroom, my mom slept quietly, so still that I could barely see her abdomen rise and fall with each breath. I held one hand of each of my girls in my own as we walked slowly toward the door.

"Come and say hello to your grandmother," I whispered at the entrance to the bedroom. Just then, I stopped in my tracks. *No, no, no. I don't want to wake her, she seems so peaceful.* The thought was like a lightening flash, quick and bright, then gone. Just as quickly came the next thought, more certain and solid. *It's okay. Now is the time.* The struggle I faced with this one simple act—to have my girls see their dying grandmother—was characteristic of my constant focus on trusting my intuition. Invariably, I have an initial thought, and then I question it before quickly deciding on the correct course of action. Over the years, I have learned to embrace this as my way of processing and acting. More times than not, it has served me well.

When the girls and I finally walked into my mother's bedroom, she was awake and had managed to sit up slightly in bed. "Come here, my little princesses," she said softly. "Come to Grandma."

My daughters went over to her bedside and embraced her, followed by kisses placed gently on her cheeks.

She said to them, "Halloween is coming up, and I wanted to go to parties and have fun with you, but I can't join you this year. But I want you to enjoy yourselves and be happy." Her voice trailed off as if something in the corner of the room had distracted her. Then, she continued, "I want you to be good daughters to your mommy the way she has been a good daughter to me. I love you all very much. Just know that everything is going to be okay."

At the bedside with my daughters, my back to them, I sobbed silently with a broken heart, hoping my daughters couldn't sense my heartache or hear my sniffles. All they knew was that grandma was in bed and that she wanted them to be happy. Being able to say goodbye to my best friend, my mother, my everything, and to have my daughters with me, was the biggest blessing and gift from God I had ever experienced and is something for which I will be eternally grateful. As the sun peeked gently through the curtains, we kissed her once more and told her we loved her. Then we left, as my brother Arthur arrived.

A few hours later, while at work, I received a call from Big Brother Joe. I knew instinctively, before he said a word, that my mother had died. I drove home in silence, the picture of my mother and my daughters fresh in my mind. I was devastated, but not emotional because she had asked me to make arrangements for her funeral. Knowing I would be responsible for fulfilling her last wishes, two weeks earlier, my intuition had kicked in and led me to the Sacred Heart Co-Cathedral, just across from my office, where I met privately with my confidant, Archbishop Joseph Fiorenza. While speaking with him about my mother's declining health, I had a complete breakdown, as if she had died that very moment. I knew this was God's way of allowing me to grieve before she actually took her last breath just two weeks later.

My mother, the person who knew me like no other, was gone. She was the one who could pep me up with a glance or a word. My mom was my world, and now she was gone. As emotionally crushed as I was, somehow, I was also grateful. Grateful for the opportunity that my daughters had to be at her bedside only hours before she passed, that her death was such a peaceful one. Grateful that my mom and I had shared so much together and had such a close relationship that nothing was left unsaid between us.

Tomasa Gonzalez

March 7, 1926—
October 28, 2011

Remember Me

Remember me when flowers bloom
Early in the spring
Remember me on sunny days
in the fun that summer brings
Remember me in the fall
As you walk through leaves of gold
And remember me in the wintertime
In the stories that are told
And most of all remember
Each day—right from the start
I will be forever near
For I live within your heart
- J. Morse

———●———

As I took the stage in the ballroom at the Hobby Center for the annual Houston Chamber of Commerce Fundraising Gala, the scene was surreal. As MC for the event, I was proud to welcome twelve hundred people to the Chamber's largest, most high-profile annual event in decades. In the week following my mom's burial, my staff and I had been in the throes of planning this elegant event, and I could not afford to ignore my responsibilities at work. So I buried myself in my work in the midst of making plans to bury my mom. As it turned out, my hard-charging work ethic kept me from being overwhelmed with sadness about her death. I had so much to do that I had to process my grief through the pauses in my activities at work and with the girls. What might have seemed to some like an unhealthy way to grieve, actually became for me the ideal environment to process my emotions without falling apart completely.

My girls joined me at the gala, and the love and support others showed us was beautiful. Taking them to the gala after my mother died was my way of showing them that there are things in life that happen that you cannot control. My mom's death was one of those things. Despite those unforeseen situations, you have to step up and live life in the present moment. In my address to the audience that night, I took a moment of personal privilege to thank everyone for their condolences on the passing of my mother and then continued with the program. My brief, simple remarks were enough to remind me of the beauty of the circle of life, to show my girls that God gave me the strength to acknowledge my mother with love, and to insulate my grief until later.

Life is about choices, and the choice I faced at that time was to either be sad that my mother had died or to appreciate the blessing of having her as my mom and being able to say goodbye to her the way I did. Her love and her life were gifts and blessings that gave me the strength and courage to thank God for blessing me with such a wonderful mom.

Just one week after my mom passed away, I took the stage and welcomed 1200 attendees at the Annual Houston Hispanic Chamber of Commerce fundraising gala.

———— ● ————

The months after my mom's death passed quickly. Before I knew it, Christmas was just weeks away, and I wanted to avoid the grief and sadness imminent for my girls and me with this, our first Christmas without the matriarch of our family. I prayed for a new and exciting experience, one we could enjoy together and that would honor the influence my mom had in our lives. Amazingly, an invitation came in the mail from the Office of the President of the United States, Barak Obama, to attend a White House Christmas celebration. This was exactly what we needed. My girls and I visited Washington that year and enjoyed the beauty of the capital and the splendor of the White House in full Christmas decor. It was the magical experience we all needed to help heal from my mom's death.

Through my work with the Chamber, I had met President Obama on several occasions. Each time, I had the opportunity to introduce myself, as did others in attendance. When everyone else would step up to shake his hand, they would say their name and the organization they represented. I, on the other hand, used each meeting to greet the president with a simple statement expressing the platform and focus of the Chamber at that time, "Houston, comprehensive immigration." With that, I would smile, look him in the eyes, shake his hand, and move on.

Having been fortunate to receive invitations to attend many national and international presidential inaugurations in Washington, DC, and throughout the world, receiving the invitation to attend a Hispanic Heritage reception was both an honor and an acknowledgment that my efforts to gain visibility for what the Houston Hispanic Chamber of Commerce was focused on had made an impression in the nation's capital.

While attending the Hispanic Heritage reception, I mingled with dignitaries and leaders from across the nation. Out of nowhere, two secret service officers approached me and asked that I step away from the gathering and come with them. Unsure of their intent, but curious as to what this was about, I followed them silently into the red room, where a dozen other national leaders were joined for a private discussion of a topic that had become a priority for the president, comprehensive immigration. When President Obama approached me in that small room, he reached out his hand to me and said, "Houston, comprehensive immigration." That night, I was ready to finally say my name, but he surprised me by repeating my line to me, as I had said it to him on so many occasions.

Blink

Caring for my mother in the last year of her life had been challenging and required a lot of strength—mentally, physically, and emotionally—to deal with her illness. With so much of my focus on helping my mother remain comfortable during her illness, I had neglected my own health. One day, I noticed a growth on the left side of my face near my ear. Although it was small, I decided to go to the doctor for an exam. Although not alarmed about the growth, the doctor instructed me to keep an eye on it and let him know of any changes. Intuitively, I knew I needed a second opinion and additional testing. Ultimately, insisting on an MRI at the Texas Medical Center saved my life.

The scan revealed that the small growth was, in fact, a tumor, and that this tumor could be dangerous and possibly cancerous. As it turned out, the growth was located near several nerve endings that control speech, hearing, blinking, and other functions. The specialist told me it needed to be removed immediately because this type of tumor was known to grow aggressively and could become even larger than my entire face.

Explaining the surgical procedure, the doctor said, "We'll cut near your ear and lift your face forward to remove the tumor, ideally without causing any damage to nerves around the tumor."

Because of the location of the tumor, there was a high possibility that my speech might be slurred, my vision might be diminished, and I might no longer be able to blink. Not being able to blink was something I had never thought about. He even mentioned that they might have to cut in the fold of my neck, which could leave significant scarring, especially along the side of my face and across my neck. As I considered all that he said, I knew immediately what was best for me.

"Doctor, I don't care about any of that," I said. "I just want to be well. I want to live. I want to be able to speak and continue to see and blink and do all the things that help me live a vibrant life. Just cut it out. Do what you have to."

The day before the surgery, I went to the hospital to check in with admissions and get registered for the following day. When my name was called by the admissions clerk, I walked over to her desk.

"Hello, please have a seat," she said. "I'll need your driver's license and insurance card."

As I ruffled through my purse to gather the items she had requested, I glanced at her name badge. "Hope," the badge read. Being a visual person, I believe in signs. Nothing is a coincidence. I always try to find the good side of any situation because it puts me in a positive mood and helps me feel better in tense situations. So when I saw her name, I was immediately curious.

"Excuse me, ma'am, is Hope really your name?" I asked, half expecting her to admit that she had chosen that word for her badge to give a sense of calm to nervous patients.

"Yes," she said, "that's actually my name."

Somehow, that was all I needed in order to believe everything would be okay. A sense of calm overcame me, similar to that calm I felt when the gun was pointed to my head all those years earlier. As she completed the admissions paperwork, I began to feel an immense sense of gratitude that I lived in a city where I had access to the world-renowned Texas Medical Center and their physicians. I left the entire matter in God's hands.

The next day, I arrived for the procedure. What was supposed to be a six-hour surgery actually lasted over nine hours because, once the doctors made the incision and identified the growth, they discovered more complicated issues. Fortunately, the surgery went well, the scarring was minimal, and the incision across my neck that the doctor initially suspected would be necessary didn't have to happen. Even more exciting was that the growth was benign.

When I woke up from the surgery, the first thing I did was blink. I could blink! Who thinks about whether they can blink? Now, every day when I wake up I blink and I am grateful to God. Hence my exuberant energy and zest for life.

Thankfully, there were no side effects of the surgery, except one. The surgeon indicated that I might periodically experience tingling at the top of my earlobe near the incision. If that was the only issue with this type of surgery, I was grateful. The surgery was performed during the Christmas break when the Chamber offices were closed, and I returned to work a week later. I never shared this potentially life-altering experience with anyone. As with the incident when my mother and I were held at gunpoint, I didn't want sympathy from others, nor did I want to allow myself to focus inadvertently on what could have been. I was alive and I was grateful for that.

Months later, for the first time, I experienced the tingling the surgeon mentioned might occur. When I first felt it, I was startled, but ever the optimist, I chose to believe this was God's way of reminding me that, yet again, he had spared my life and that life is to be lived with passion. I am convinced my exuberant energy comes from knowing my life has been spared several times. Life is short, and being constantly grateful for this life where I am focused on getting things done and serving others is what motivates me each day. In the years since the surgery, every now and again, when I feel that tingling sensation, I am overwhelmed with gratitude and reinvigorated to serve others.

Pitch from the Mound

I had never thrown a baseball—well, not until I was invited to throw the ceremonial pitch at a Houston Astros game in 2016. There I was on the field of Minute Maid Park, home of the Astros, the stadium full of raving fans awaiting the conclusion of the pregame festivities, cameras set to snap the perfect shot. Standing in blue pants and white blouse with matching leather pumps, I was ready. Behind me stood the pitcher, as if there for emotional support. He approached me and said in a kind voice, "Ma'am, don't worry, you can get closer. You don't have to pitch from the mound."

The spirit of his reassuring words came through in his gentle voice, and although I appreciated the gesture, I thought, *He doesn't know me.* The invitation to throw the ceremonial pitch had come on two separate occasions, thanks to the relationships I had built with the Astros. The easy thing for me to have done was take the pitcher's advice, move forward several steps, and toss the ball like an amateur. As a woman, I know I have to be ready to step up to the plate, use my knowledge and skills, practice, and be prepared, just as any man would. Lowering the standards, changing the rules, or providing special circumstances to assist in my success were not options for me. I have never expected that in any aspect of my life, and I didn't expect it at that moment.

"Thanks, that's kind of you," I said with a smile. "I'm good. I'll pitch from the mound."

In the days leading up to that game, I experienced alternating feelings of excitement and intimidation at the prospect of standing center field before a crowd of fans for a televised baseball game. I didn't even know how to hold a baseball properly, much less pitch one. So I enlisted University of Houston-Downtown student Manny Rojas, who had played baseball for many years.

"Manny, I've been asked by the Astros to toss the ceremonial pitch at the next game." I explained. "I have to at least look like I know what I'm doing. I need your help. Tomorrow, would you go with me to the park and let me pitch the ball to you, maybe give me some pointers?"

As a leader, I can't know everything, but I can surround myself with others who know what I don't know. Asking for help with things other people know how to do better than I do has become critical to my success. Having worked with extremely dedicated and intelligent bosses throughout my career, I have been blessed to have learned so much from them. Therefore, I have learned to value the experience and acuity of others when trying something new.

Manny smiled and said, "Sure, Dr. Murillo. I'd be glad to." Then, he gave me a quick once over and raised one eyebrow. "But, you're going to change shoes, aren't you?"

"No. Why would I practice in tennis shoes?" I asked. "I'm going to pitch in heels!"

The next day, Manny and I went to the park to toss some balls. He was so patient with me, and his tips helped improve my pitch tremendously. That gave me the confidence I needed to believe I could actually go out on the field and step up to the plate.

Throwing the ceremonial first pitch at two different Houston Astros games.

What I didn't know is that during the pregame there is more than one ceremonial first pitch. Prior to me stepping onto the pitcher's mound that day, two men took turns throwing the first pitch. The first guy was a stud and threw the ball like a pro. Needless to say, I was intimidated. The next guy listened intently to the pitcher's advice and stepped off the mound to walk closer to the catcher before tossing the ball. His pitch was horrible. *Okay, maybe I have a fighting chance here.* By then, the crowd was dying, anxious to get the game going, and then, I walked out. As I carefully stepped up to the mound, I was reminded that throughout my life, people have underestimated me. Whether because I am a woman or because I am Hispanic or because I was younger than they expected, I'm not sure, and I've never wasted much time trying to figure that out. In all those situations where I was underestimated, I somehow found the gumption to show up big and do my best.

That day, I knew that practically everyone in that stadium underestimated me. They were probably betting on my failure to pitch the ball with any semblance of accuracy. But the stadium fell silent when I thanked the pitcher, waved my hand to refuse his offer, and turned to face the catcher. I was ready. With the ball held tightly between my first two fingers and my thumb, I loosely held the knuckles of my outer fingers against the ball. With a steeled glance ahead, I began my wind-up, arms outstretched, then raised over my head, knee up, chest out, big inhale, and quick release.

The ball shot out straight and fast. The crowd's applause muffled the sound of the ball sinking into the catcher's mitt, but I knew it had connected and I felt great. Success!

In conversations with women's groups—whether professional presentations or intimate conversations with young women in a mentoring role—I show them the video of my ceremonial pitch at the Astros game. I share with them the inside story of what led up to that moment. They need to know I was scared, I was nervous, and yet, I was determined. They can relate, and they can also appreciate that I prepared and pushed through the fear. I was determined to pitch from the mound, and I encourage the same determination from them.

DIVERSITY BY DESIGN

Life doesn't have to make exceptions for you just because you are different. No one owes you a special place on the team or an easy way in or out. Roman philosopher Seneca said, "Luck is what happens when preparation meets opportunity." I say success happens when preparation meets opportunity. You don't have to change who you are to succeed. You just have to prepare.

Prepare for every opportunity. In fact, over-prepare. Draw upon whatever level of confidence you can muster. Get help, even from someone younger than you. And then, step up to life's opportunities and pitch from the mound.

Be Ready and Stay Ready

Some people are born with an undeniable confidence in everything they do. They step up to the line and are ready whenever an opportunity presents itself. My youngest daughter, Mia, is like that. But even the most confident among us can sometimes be intimidated by difficult circumstances and get discouraged when the rules are changed or the odds are stacked against them.

At seven years old, Mia was among four girls who played on her school's co-ed basketball team. Early on, she enjoyed it, but as the season progressed, the boys on the team would hog the ball. It became frustrating to the girls, who were as good as the boys but never had a chance to show their skills because of how selfishly the boys played. At each game, there was one less girl on the court because they were dropping out, frustrated at not having an equal chance to demonstrate their skill. What the coaches and the boys on the team didn't realize is that by not presenting a fair opportunity for all the players to perform at their best, they were threatening the outcomes for the entire team. The same is true inside many companies.

One evening after basketball practice, Mia came home and said,

DIVERSITY BY DESIGN

Creating an equitable workplace environment means each person who has earned their way into the organization has an equal chance to perform to their own highest standard. There are no assumptions or distractions that enter into the equation as to whether each person can live up to their role because everyone involved knows fair due diligence has already been performed, ensuring that everyone at the table belongs there.

When artificial barriers are erected to prevent team members from entering the room, having a seat at the table, speaking up, being heard, or demonstrating their value, the culture of equity is threatened, and the negative results trickle into every aspect of the organization.

"Mom, I don't want to play anymore. The boys are mean, and now it's only me and Carey on the team with them. All the other girls quit." Her disappointment was obvious.

"Why are the girls quitting?" I asked.

"Because the boys are mean and they don't pass the ball," she replied.

At that moment, the spirit of my dad seemed to enter me and I could hear his voice in my mind, except it came out of my mouth. I said, "Mia, you will not let those little boys kick you off this team. That's what they want." Her head dropped in disappointment. I could tell she wanted me to agree with her so she could just quit the team and do something else, but I wasn't going to let her give up on herself so easily. I continued, "Instead, you will show up to practice and you will practice harder. And you know what, Mia, one day, somebody is going to pass the ball to you. When they pass the ball, you're going to shoot the ball." She glanced at me, her eyes rolling upward. "Mia, what are you going to do?"

With a big huff, she said, "Shoot the ball?"

That was the least convincing statement I had ever heard, so I asked again. "What are you going to do?"

Slightly louder, she said, "I'm gonna shoot the ball."

Still not satisfied, I asked a third time, my voice louder with each word. "Mia, what are you going to do when someone passes the ball?"

"I'm going to shoot the ball!"

By the final game of the season, Mia was ready. We had used that one simple question, repeated daily, to boost her confidence so she would know exactly what to do when the ball was passed to her, whenever that might be. With just Mia and Carey as the only girls left on the team, the game began. I sat under the basketball goal, my eyes focused on Mia the entire game. For the first half and into the second half of the game, Mia hadn't even touched the ball. No one would pass it to her. The game was close, and by the last ten seconds, our team was down by one point.

One of the boys had the ball. The other boys yelled for him to throw them the ball, but they were all covered. Mia, however, was open. *Ten, nine, eight, seven.* I yelled, "Mia, get the ball!" The kid with the ball didn't know what to do. Just as he was about to throw the ball to another guy, he saw Mia open, waving her arms. *Six, five, four.* In the heat of the moment, he passed the ball to Mia. Without the time to think about the false assumptions his teammates had practiced throughout the season, that kid realized winning was more important than keeping the lone girl on the court out of the game. In a nanosecond, she caught the ball, and I could almost see her mouth the words we had been practicing. *What will you do when they pass the ball, Mia? Shoot the ball.* "Shoot the ball, Mia!" I yelled.

Three, two, one. Swish. She shot the ball and scored the winning basket. Her teammates, all the boys who refused to allow her to play earlier in the season, lifted her up in celebration of the win.

Confidence. That experience was all about having the confidence to step up and shoot the ball, even when others don't believe in your ability. Whether at the board table or in a game, believing you belong and having the confidence to act are invaluable skills that must be practiced time and again, particularly for people in marginalized groups or who represent the minority in a situation. Being prepared and showing up are the most essential tasks. Just one experience of catching the ball of opportunity and shooting it for the win can change the trajectory of your life. Today, Mia is one of the most confident people I know. At age sixteen, she became the youngest congressional intern in the 2018 cohort. She also went on to become the first Hispanic to earn the highly coveted St. John's School Headmaster's Award, the highest honor bestowed upon a student by the school.

DIVERSITY BY DESIGN

Organizations need not wait for impossible situations to test team members' ability to perform at their best. Every day offers endless opportunities for companies to demonstrate a culture of equity by allowing people to shine. Walking the talk of equity means seeing everyone for the potential they bring and leveling the field so everyone has the resources and support to be their best. And remember to acknowledge and celebrate the accomplishments of each team member.

My daughter, Mia earned the St. John's School Headmaster Award becoming the first Latina to earn the highest honor bestowed by the school.

Mia earned the Maverick Award for upholding the St. John's school precepts, the highest honor bestowed by the school — the Headmaster Award (selected by faculty), the Upper School Literary Award, the Garwood Award for U.S. History, and she was a Princeton University Race Relations finalist.

Own Your Seat at the Table

Many times in my life, I have had to muster the confidence and stand in the truth that if I was invited to the table, there was a role for me to play. I needed to know what that role was, show up prepared, and be ready to own my seat at the table.

Thanks to Mark Montgomery, BBVA CEO, for asking me to serve on the BBVA Houston advisory board. My role on the board—composed mostly of men who had been in banking or related careers for many decades and had long-standing relationships in Houston and River Oaks—caused me to feel a bit intimidated. There I was, one of only three women serving in that capacity, looking around the table and asking myself what I could contribute to help the bank move forward in the direction the board was discussing. Oftentimes, women doubt ourselves and our contributions to the conversation. Some of us suffer from imposter syndrome or other confidence issues, and therefore we miss opportunities to add our voices and experiences to the conversations about critical measures to move a company forward. Through many experiences like this, I have learned to push aside those feelings of inadequacy and be confident in the value I bring to the table.

DIVERSITY BY DESIGN

A report by the Society for Human Resources Management indicated that white individuals account for about 60 percent of the population but hold 84 percent of Fortune 500 board seats. Latinos, the country's fastest-growing ethnicity, make up 18.5 of the population, but fill just 2.2 percent of board seats on Russell 3000 companies' boards. And Black individuals represent 12.5 percent of the population but hold just 4.1 percent of Russell 3000 board seats. In addition, 37 percent of S&P 500 companies had no Black board members in 2019 (Society for Human Resources Management, "Corporate Board Diversity: Moving Beyond Lip Service," January 16, 2021, by June D. Bell).

As I pushed those confidence issues aside, I reminded myself that I had information about small business as it related to employment, mortgages, and other areas of interest to the bank's growth. Once I realized this, my confidence grew, and I reached out to other board members to learn a bit about them and how I could use my influence to assist them in their areas of specialty. I went from being fearful and wondering why I was there to feeling empowered and knowing my experience and my knowledge were valuable. I aligned myself with other board members and invited them to different events or programs so they could see me in action outside of those BBVA board meetings. With that, we each gained a greater knowledge of and respect for each other's experience and value to the board.

In 2016, the Greater Houston Partnership (GHP) hosted a trade mission to Cuba, led by Mayor Sylvester, Houston Texans President, Jamey Rootes, and GHP President, Bob Harvey.

In 2016, I traveled to Havana, Cuba with Houston Mayor Sylvester Turner and the Greater Houston Partnership, a delegation of business leaders seeking to build alliances with their counterparts in Cuba in the areas of energy and health. As one of only two women in the delegation, on this particular trip, I believed my presence was especially significant and valuable. I was proud to have expanded the Chamber's platform beyond a Hispanic emphasis in Houston, to be more international and business focused. I had traveled across the globe with several mayors to

Brazil, Venezuela, Chile, Peru, China, Turkey, Mexico, and many other nations as a representative of similar business delegations.

One thing always present in my mind was to be ready to shoot the ball whenever it was passed to me. On this trip, I flew with about twenty-five men from a private hangar in Houston to Havana to meet with the local business and government officials. This was my first time there, and I found the city both beautiful and curious, a place where time seems to have stood still in the 1960s, while the city has also become lost in time due to the mounting needs for infrastructure improvements.

In a meeting with the mayor of Havana there were three male speakers, all sharing what a diverse city Houston was and the opportunities to do business in our city. As I sat there and glanced around the room, I realized the only other women in the room happened to be the two who were serving some refreshments, one who had set up the room for us, and an assistant to the mayor of Havana, who was taking notes and translating. The irony of the moment wasn't lost on me. There I was, a daughter of immigrant parents, sitting in Cuba with a delegation of businessmen trying to bring business from Cuba to Houston.

As I listened to the conversation in English being translated into Spanish, I noted there were some losses in translation, as there would be when trying to convey a message from one language to another. Suddenly, as if reading my mind, Mayor Turner realized there was an opportunity in the room that had been overlooked. He glanced at me and I at him. He quickly shifted the agenda and invited me to speak.

"Dr. Murillo is here," he said. "She represents over forty percent of Houston's population, Hispanics who live, work, and do business in our city. I believe the experiences and information she has will be very beneficial to those of you in this room." Just like that, he passed the ball. And just like Mia, I was prepared to shoot the ball.

In my royal blue suit, I stood up, thanked the mayor, and greeted our Cuban hosts in Spanish. Being very conscious that my presence as a woman in a formal business meeting in Cuba had very different cultural implications than in the U.S., I was aware of my body language and the respect that our Cuban hosts expected.

Greater Houston Partnership and City of Houston trade delegation in Havana, Cuba.
(Left to Right) GHP President Bob Harvey, GHP Chairman Jamey Rootes, Mayor Sylvester
Turner, and Havana's Mayor.

I talked about the value of expanding international business partnerships between our countries. The representatives from Cuba were impressed and told me so. I was grateful that Mayor Turner recognized an opportunity to acknowledge the diversity of our group by inviting me to participate both as a woman and as a Spanish-speaking delegate. His decision that day elevated my role among the group for the remainder of the trip.

This was one of several such international trips I have taken during my tenure as CEO of the Chamber that afforded me the opportunity to travel with the mayor and experience how different cultures interact and how tied we all are to each other's economies and cultures. These trips expanded my international scope and perspective and allowed me to promote Houston to the world. Above all, I learned the value of stepping out of my own space and going into someone else's, always ready to shoot the ball.

CHAPTER 6

MY HOUR OF INSPIRATION

For me, 3:00 a.m. seems to be my hour of inspiration, the time when my creativity kicks in and innovative ideas come to life. Waking up often at this hour became a reality for me in my early thirties, and back then, it was irritating. I didn't see this early morning wake-up call as a blessing. Because I always had so much going on in my long days, I wanted to sleep later, assuming more sleep would rejuvenate and energize me. In fact, occasionally waking early has become my energy source. I now embrace my hour of inspiration and look forward to all the new ideas and strategies I will develop.

During this hour of inspiration, my mind seems to relax, allowing clarity on things that have become lost in the busy-ness of the day. It is then that I can connect the dots and visualize what I might have missed throughout the day. Typically, I get a flood of questions, and I have learned to get out my notebook and write things down. There are no bad ideas. I just put pen to paper and write. One thing leads to another, and I begin to review every detail of the previous day, from beginning to end. Then I ask, "What could make that experience or that project better? How can I improve on it next time? What can I add or remove to make it better?" This is how ideas are advanced.

Doing everything well is important to me. When I share my ambitions with others who support me, I have a greater sense of accountability, even when I have feelings of fear or when I question my confidence. Once I face my fears, doubts, and concerns, I am able to move forward with the confidence that I can accomplish what I set out to do. The fear is still there, but I take deliberate action, one step at a time, one thing at a time, one call at a time, and one conversation at a time.

I liken my hour of inspiration to the training schedule of a high-performance athlete who knows what it takes to consistently improve and be the best. They wake up early, exercise daily, eat well, and train. These actions can be painful, daunting, and challenging. This is what the fans and the outside world never see. When that athlete steps onto the field wearing their uniform, they're smiling and waving at the cameras. When they step up to the plate and hit that home run, it's beautiful. The crowd is mesmerized by their skill and talent because it looks easy, seamless. They should be mesmerized because the skill and talent, coupled with the training, is what they see. Sheer poetry in motion. But the athlete knows there is more to it than that single swing.

Only a select few people know the backstory of the body aches and the personal disappointments when they didn't play their best. That is all part of success. The fans see the beauty and the win, but the dedicated athlete knows what it takes to get there. It takes commitment, working with urgency, having passion, and training with persistence. Success is the result of working hard in order to excel. Like the athlete, I set a very high level of expectation for myself and the outcomes I want to accomplish. Working at a high level of engagement is a choice. When I need to slow down or disconnect, I do so because I know I need to reset. I have been fortunate to surround myself with people who encourage me to reset, to get away and take a break. Even as I reset and recharge, my mind is continuously solving problems and formulating questions. Because of that, this process of early morning review and revision is not done out of frustration or negative feelings. Instead, it is done from a place of passion, interest, improvement, and personal achievement.

When most people see high achievers doing their thing, making deals, accomplishing goals, impacting others, they see the outcomes and the results, and that's fine. However, when I see successful people, I tend to focus on what is not seen, what's beneath the surface. To me, that is where the lessons lie. The opportunities to learn from these people have a lot more to do with what is unseen—the challenges, the illnesses, the time commitments, the guilt of working and not spending enough time with family and friends, and the constant engagement in projects in service to others—all the sacrifices they make to succeed. They are fulfilled because they have accomplished their goals.

I strive to over-achieve and exceed expectations. When others underestimate me, I use that as a motivator. In fact, I count myself lucky when someone says it can't be done. That is my green light to move forward with passion and persistence, to work with urgency, and to both prove them wrong and also prove to myself that I can achieve anything I set my mind to doing. I am grateful to all the people who have been a part of my journey, the believers and supporters, and those who underestimated me. Despite and because of them all, my journey continues because there is much more to accomplish.

By the sheer tenacity of my parents, who left their homeland of Mexico and crossed the Rio Grande as immigrants in the hope for a better life for themselves, I am here. Whenever I think of my parents, I am grateful for the sacrifices they made to make sure their nine children would be able to live the American dream, that every sacrifice they made was to provide an opportunity for their children to live better lives.

With every challenge I face in my career or personally, I am reminded that, no matter how difficult or challenging my experiences were, my parents' challenges were much more daunting than mine. In a country where dreams were meant to be lived and realized, the power of visualization and the power of dreaming big, executing on dreams, and taking steps to reach them, is in my DNA.

I hope that as you have read this book, you've been inspired and motivated to see signs as friendly reminders in your life that you have something to contribute and things to do. Whether a tingle on your earlobe, a single rose in a crystal vase, a box of tomatoes, a knitting needle, or a basketball hoop, be aware of life's signs and signals, and commit yourself to live life to the fullest every day because, as I have been reminded on more than one occasion, life can be gone in the blink of an eye, the pull of a trigger, or the gasp of a final breath.

Thanks to those extreme life incidents, I have dedicated my life to utilizing all the gifts God has bestowed upon me for good. That is how I lead in life.

My parents, my heroes, Tomasa and José González.

ABOUT THE AUTHOR

In 2007, Dr. Laura Murillo was named President and CEO of the Houston Hispanic Chamber of Commerce. Under her leadership, the Chamber has set unprecedented records in membership and revenue, becoming one of the most influential Chambers in the nation. Just two years after taking the helm, Murillo, the Board of Directors, and dedicated staff won the National and Regional Hispanic Chamber of the Year Award from the U.S. Hispanic Chamber of Commerce. Throughout her exceptional leadership of the Chamber, the organization has continued to receive recognition—including Marketer of the Year by the American Marketing Association three times, and two Diversity in Business Awards from the *Houston Business Journal*—a clear testament to her exceptional leadership.

Dr. Murillo is the Founding President and CEO of the Greater Houston Hispanic Chamber of Commerce Foundation. During her tenure, the Emerging Leaders Institute was established and has celebrated over three hundred graduates. She is the Founding Executive Producer/Host of the Chamber's radio and television programs on CBS (KHOU 11 and QuestTEXAS), Audacy, Univision, and the KUBE-57 with a cumulative audience reach of 3.3 million. She is also a commentator on national media outlets.

She holds a B.A., a Master's Degree, and a Doctorate from the University of Houston, where she served as an executive for fifteen years and became the youngest Director in UH history. The University of Houston bestowed its highest honor, the President's Medallion, to the Chamber and Dr. Murillo. Prior to her current role, she served as an Executive at Memorial Hermann-Texas Medical Center for seven years and served on the CEO's Executive Committee, where she was accountable for a $300 million budget, 500+ employees, and ten departments.

In 2021, she was admitted into the Harvard University Women on Corporate Boards Executive Program.

She was named among *Texas CEO Magazine*'s Top 30 Texas CEOs during COVID-19 for exceptional leadership in 2020, and was featured in *Global InfluenceMagazine*'s Championing the Success of Women in the Workplace. In 2018, she was named *Houston Business Journal's* "Most Admired CEO", "Distinguished Alumni Award" by the University of Houston, and "Mother of the Year" by the Houston Latin American Philharmonic. She has received many state, national, and international honors including being named among the "Most Powerful and Influential Women in Texas" and the "Top Latino Leader Award" by the National Diversity Council, 2017 "Power 25 Houston Award" by Walker's Legacy, "Woman of the Year" by *Success Magazine*, the "International Leadership Award" by Texas Women's Empowerment Foundation, CKW LUXE "Top 20 Impact Maker Honoree", the "Outstanding Community Service Award" by the Hispanic Bar Association of Houston, the "Global Impact Award" by Global Seven, the 2019 Civil Liberties & Justice Award, "2020 Women in History Honoree" by SSLW, and "2021 Global Leader of Influence Honoree" by the World Affairs Council.

Dr. Murillo was featured in the *Houston Chronicle*'s 2016 "Women Who Run Houston" article, and was named as "Outstanding Service Honoree" by the Mexican-American Bar Association of Texas Foundation. The National MBA Organization honored her with the "Excellence Award" and D-mars.com named her as an "Icon Honoree." She was also named "Top 10 Who's Who in Business" and has been named among the "Top 5 C-Suite CEOs" by the *Houston Business Journal*. In 2014, she was honored with the "Hispanic Leadership Award" by the National Football League (NFL).

The Ohtli Award—the highest honor bestowed by the Mexican government to a Mexican American—was awarded to Dr. Murillo for her advocacy and civic leadership in 2016. She has been included at several U.S. Presidential Inaugurations and most recently accepted an inaugural invitation from Mexico's President Andres Manuel Lopez Obrador. Several Houston mayors have included Dr. Murillo on international business delegations to Brazil, Turkey, China, Mexico, Cuba, Argentina, Peru, Chile, and other countries.

Dr. Murillo is the first Houstonian to be appointed to the Washington, DC Board of Governors of the Federal Reserve System Community Advisory Council (CAC), which has national public policy implications. Additionally, she serves on the Federal Reserve Bank of Dallas Business and Community Advisory Council, the Houston BBVA Board of Directors, the University of Houston Board of Advisors, the University of Houston College of Medicine Committee, the University of Texas MD Anderson Cancer Center Board of Visitors, Port Houston's (The International Port of Texas) Business Equity Founding Advisory Council, the Texas Southern University Chairman and President's Council, the Mayor's Hispanic Advisory Board, Avangard Corporation Board of Directors, Mayor's Hire Houston Board, Co-Chair for the Harris County International Committee, the Harris County-Houston Sports Authority Executive Committee, the Houston Super Bowl Committee, the Houston Symphony Advisory Board, the Greater Houston Convention & Visitors Bureau Board, the Kinder Institute's Kinder Houston Area Survey Advisory Board, the Friends of the American Latino Museum Committee, St. John's School Audit & Finance Committee, the U.S. Global Leadership Coalition's Advisory Committee, the Houston Stronger Coalition, the 2026 FIFA World Cup Houston Bid Committee, the Mayor's Task Force on Policing Reform, and Rice Management Company, Workforce Development.

The youngest of nine children, Laura Murillo was born to Mexican immigrant parents and was raised in Houston's East End/Magnolia, where she began working at age ten at her family's restaurant. She is the proud mother of Marisa and Mia, both honors graduates of St. John's School in River Oaks. Marisa earned a mechanical engineering degree from Columbia University in New York City and is an astrophysics researcher. Mia is a sophomore at Georgetown University in Washington, DC where she maintains highest honors.

Dr. Murillo is an international presenter who has been a keynote speaker for numerous multinational corporations including Coca-Cola, Sysco, AT&T, and Shell, to name a few. These global entities have benefitted from her insights on DEI and other topics, as well as her profound and intuitive approach to leadership development.

DrLauraMurillo.com

CPSIA information can be obtained
at www.ICGtesting.com
Printed in the USA
BVHW051548230322
631458BV00013BA/17/J